ALL ABOUT
COOKIES

ALL ABOUT
COOKIES

IRMA S. ROMBAUER
MARION ROMBAUER BECKER
ETHAN BECKER

PHOTOGRAPHY BY TUCKER & HOSSLER

SCRIBNER
NEW YORK • LONDON • TORONTO • SYDNEY • SINGAPORE

SCRIBNER
1230 Avenue of the Americas
New York, NY 10020

WELDON OWEN INC.
Chief Executive Officer: John Owen
President: Terry Newell
Chief Operating Officer: Larry Partington
Vice President, International Sales: Stuart Laurence
Publisher: Roger Shaw
Creative Director: Gaye Allen
Associate Publisher: Val Cipollone
Senior Editor: Sarah Lemas
Associate Editor: Anna Mantzaris
Consulting Editor: Barbara Ottenhoff
Art Director: Catherine Jacobes
Designers: Sarah Gifford, Lisa Schulz
Photo Editor: Lisa Lee
Production Manager: Chris Hemesath
Shipping and Production Coordinator: Libby Temple
Production: Joan Olson
Food Stylists: Kim Konecny, Erin Quon
Assistant Food Stylist: Dina Rao
Step-by-Step Photographer: Mike Falconer
Step-by-Step Food Stylist: Andrea Lucich

Joy of Cooking All About series was designed
and produced by Weldon Owen Inc.,
814 Montgomery Street, San Francisco,
California 94133

Set in Joanna MT and Gill Sans

Separations by Bright Arts Singapore
Printed in Singapore by Tien Wah Press (Pte.) Ltd.

10 9 8 7 6 5 4 3 2 1

Library of Congress Cataloging-in-Publication Data
Rombauer, Irma von Starkloff, 1877-1962.
   Joy of cooking. All about cookies/Irma S. Rombauer,
Marion Rombauer Becker, Ethan Becker.
     p. cm
   Includes index.
   ISBN 0-7432-1680-6
   1. Cookies. I. Title: All about cookies. II. Becker,
Marion Rombauer. III. Becker, Ethan. IV. Title.
TX772 .R649 2002
641.8'654—dc21
                                    2001020957

Recipes shown on half-title page: *Chocolate Chip Icebox
Cookies* and *Icebox Sugar Cookies*, 110
Recipe shown on title page: *Mother Kroll's Lebkuchen*, 55

CONTENTS

6   FOREWORD

8   ABOUT **COOKIES**

21   ABOUT **DROP** COOKIES

39   ABOUT **BAR** COOKIES

59   ABOUT **ROLLED** COOKIES

73   ABOUT **HAND-SHAPED** COOKIES

97   ABOUT **FILLED** COOKIES

109   ABOUT **SLICED, PIPED & PRESSED** COOKIES

126   INDEX

128   ACKNOWLEDGMENTS

FOREWORD

"Kids and cookies are inseparable," my Granny Rom used to say. Like my mom, who often repeated that phrase, I certainly agree. Based on a lifetime of baking cookies—not to mention eating cookies—I would also like to add that cookies bring out the kid in all of us.

The pleasure that people of all ages find in bite-sized baked goods is reason enough to devote an entire volume of the new All About series to cookies. As you look through the pages, you'll also discover that, easy though cookies are to make, there's a lot to learn about the different ways to mix, flavor, shape, bake, and decorate them. The result is a limitless variety of delights you can share with family and friends.

You might notice that this collection of kitchen-tested recipes is adapted from the latest edition of the Joy of Cooking. Just as our family has done for generations, we have worked to make this version of Joy a little bit better than the last. As a result, you'll find that some notes, recipes, and techniques have been changed to improve their clarity and usefulness. Since 1931, the Joy of Cooking has constantly evolved. And now, the All About series has taken Joy to a whole new stage, as you will see from the beautiful color photographs of finished treats and clearly illustrated instructions for preparing and enjoying them. Granny Rom and Mom would have been delighted.

I'm sure you'll find All About Cookies to be both a useful and an enduring companion in your kitchen.

Enjoy!

Ethan Becker pictured with his grandmother, Irma von Starkloff Rombauer (left), and his mother, Marion Rombauer Becker (right). Irma Rombauer published the first Joy of Cooking at her own expense in 1931. Marion Rombauer Becker became coauthor in 1951. Joy as it has progressed through the decades (from top left to bottom right): the 1931 edition with Marion's depiction of St. Martha of Bethany, said to be the patron saint of cooking, "slaying the dragon of kitchen drudgery"; the 1943 edition; the 1951 edition; the 1962 edition; the 1975 edition; and the 1997 edition.

About Cookies

The smell of cookies baking is one of life's most satisfying pleasures. Making cookies at home is so popular because it is so easy. Once you know a few simple secrets, they require only very basic ingredients, equipment, and techniques.

The best cookies are made from the best ingredients. Use unsalted butter, and don't stint. If possible, use unsalted nuts, and make sure that they're very fresh. (Nuts are oily, and the oil can turn rancid with age.) Dried fruits such as raisins, dates, and candied citrus bits should always be plump and moist; hard, dried-out "bullets" not only are untoothsome, but also will draw off moisture and make cookies dry. Don't economize on baking chocolate or on spices. Believe it or not, there is a dramatic difference between the flavor of genuine cinnamon and that of ground cassia, often sold as a cinnamon substitute. Always buy pure vanilla, almond, or other extracts, not imitation, which can taste tinny and artificial.

Always use large eggs when baking. Their size is closely regulated for uniformity, one large egg weighing 2 ounces in the shell and 1.75 ounces out of the shell. It is important to note that an egg is a liquid ingredient and substituting extra-large or jumbo eggs will throw off the balance of a recipe.

Baking, unlike some other kinds of cooking, is not a casually improvisational art. Unable to taste, correct, and create along the way, the baker is a stickler for measurements, insistent on proper pans, and fussy about the temperature of everything from the oven to the butter.

Read each recipe through before starting, always preheat the oven for 20 minutes before baking, and measure out all the ingredients carefully before you start mixing them.

A cookie must have certain characteristics to earn it a place in the home-baking hall of fame: a distinctive texture, be it brittle-crisp, chewy-gooey, crunchy, silky, or melt-in-the-mouth (great cookies are rarely dry or cakey); an inviting appearance—which is not to say necessarily a picture-perfect one; a size and shape suitable to the cookie's character (oversize and sturdy for munching from a baggy in a lunch box, say, or dainty and chic for perching on a saucer at a tea); and most of all, of course, good flavor.

Measuring Ingredients and Mixing Cookies

While most cookie recipes are fairly forgiving, you will achieve consistent results by measuring accurately. For dry ingredients such as flour and sugar, use dry measuring cups in the exact increments you are measuring. Level the ingredients by sweeping a knife across the top of the cup. Measure small quantities of dry ingredients, such as leavenings, with measuring spoons, precisely leveled off. Use clear measuring cups marked off in increments for measuring liquids. Check the level of the liquid at eye level.

The method used to mix a dough is directly related to the texture of the finished cookie. Cookies can be made with an electric mixer, in a food processor, or by hand with a wooden spoon. Sometimes a recipe directs kneading the cookie dough. This should be done by hand.

Unless otherwise specified, it's best to let butter, flour, eggs, nuts, and other ingredients warm up almost to room temperature before using. If a recipe calls for "softened" butter, make sure it's not too cold and firm (which will make it too stiff and lumpy to fluff up or "cream" properly) or nearly melted (which will make it too thin to fluff up at all). If the butter is too cold or too warm, it can even change the temperature of the dough enough to significantly alter baking time. Once you add flour to the wet ingredients in a recipe, don't overbeat the dough; this can develop the gluten in the flour, resulting in tough cookies.

WARMING INGREDIENTS

To transform cold dairy products into room-temperature ingredients (68° to 70°F) quickly, use the microwave, a few seconds at a time, on low power. Break eggs and separate or beat them lightly before microwaving, and stir before checking the temperature each time. Butter should feel malleable but firm.

Reduced-Fat Cookies

Because some fat is essential for flavor, tenderness, proper crisping, and browning in almost every kind of cookie (meringue kisses are a rare exception), we've significantly reduced fat without eliminating it entirely in the cookies marked (Reduced Fat). Cookies that might originally have contained 4 to 8 grams of fat apiece now contain 1½ to 3½—enough to maintain good flavor and an attractive texture. We've also de-emphasized butter in favor of canola and corn oil. Some butter is usually needed to produce a manageable consistency and a hint of buttery taste, however, so we've left in a little bit.

Please don't be tempted to substitute low-fat margarine or "spread" for butter, since these products tend to have a high water content, which can turn cookie dough runny and yield a flattened-out and overdone end result. If you insist on avoiding butter, use regular nondiet stick margarine instead. You'll lose some flavor, but at least the consistency should be right. Wherever possible, our reduced-fat recipes also cut down on the number of egg yolks used. If a recipe does call for egg yolks, though, it's because they're essential for tenderness or flavor.

It is particularly important not to overbeat reduced-fat cookies, as this can turn lean doughs tough. Pay close attention to recommended baking times, too, and remove cookies from the oven the instant they're done, as lower fat means less moisture and these cookies can dry out quickly.

INGREDIENTS AND SUBSTITUTIONS

Quite satisfactory results can be obtained by replacing up to half the butter with the same amount of regular nondiet stick margarine in the recipes. Do not substitute margarine for butter in shortbreads or butter cookies, though, because the flavor of these cookies depends so much on a truly buttery richness. Bleached flour produces a more tender, buttery cookie than unbleached flour, and has a less wheaty flavor. If you like to use whole-wheat flour, start with highly flavored cookies (those with molasses or chocolate, for instance), and replace no more than a third of the all-purpose flour with whole-wheat flour. If you can find it, whole-wheat pastry flour is best. However, cookies made even with this whole-wheat flour will always be slightly darker and heavier than the all-purpose-flour variety.

Baking Cookies

Preheating the oven: Always turn the oven on at least 20 minutes before baking.

Pans: Use medium- to heavy-gauge, shiny, rimless metal cookie sheets. They are specifically designed so that heat can circulate evenly over the cookies. Dark sheets may cause over-browning or burning. A pan with high sides will both obstruct the flow of heat and make the cookies difficult to remove. Cookie sheets come in many sizes. But for most modern ovens, sheets in the 17 x 14-inch range are perfect. They can accommodate 12 to 16 medium cookies.

If your cookies burn on the bottom, even with shiny sheets, the first thing to do is invest in an oven thermometer to make sure the oven's setting and the interior temperature agree. It is surprising how many ovens are off in one direction or the other—sometimes by as much as 30 or 40 degrees! If this is not the problem, the most economical approach is to try double panning—baking with one sheet on top of another. If this does not work, the final step might be buying very heavy-gauge pans or ones with an air-cushion inset, shown opposite.

Preparing cookie sheets: Unless a recipe gives other instructions, always grease baking sheets with butter or shortening or coat with nonstick spray. Several varieties of cookies—shortbreads and other kinds that contain no eggs but have a high percentage of fat, for instance—can be baked on un-greased sheets. And a few, such as meringue kisses and others with a large proportion of egg whites and little or no fat, will stick tenaciously unless baked on parchment paper or on generously greased and floured cookie sheets.

Unless your oven is very large and your cookie sheets very small, bake only one sheet of cookies at a time. If you do bake more than one sheet at once, make sure the sheets are identical. Do not bake partial sheets of cookies, and do not leave large gaps between cookies; doing either may affect spreading, brown-ing, crisping, and baking time. If there is only enough dough left for a few cookies, switch to a very small baking sheet, a 12-inch pizza pan, or an inverted metal pie pan, so the cookies can be spaced the required distance apart. This will ensure that the heat from the pan is absorbed

evenly and that the amount of dough is right for the baking surface. Unless otherwise noted, position a rack in the center of the oven to accommodate one baking sheet. When a recipe specifies baking in the upper, middle, or lower third of the oven, be sure to follow instructions. Finally, rotate the cookie sheets halfway through baking, turning them front to back, to ensure even browning. (Note: This is repeated in those cookie recipes where it is especially important.)

Timing: Many factors can affect baking time, so a range of suggested times is given in the recipes that follow. Always set your kitchen timer to the minimum time specified; it's easy to reset it and bake longer if necessary, but once a pan is forgotten and cookies are overbaked or burned, there is no remedy.

Removing cookies from sheets to cool: When the cookies are done, remove the cookie sheet from the oven immediately. As soon as the cookies can be moved without crumbling or tearing, gently lift them one at a time with a wide, fine-bladed spatula and place them

flat on racks until completely cool. Usually this will be in a minute or two, but it is a good idea to check by trying to lift a test cookie with a spatula every 30 seconds or so. Very tender, short cookies (those containing a lot of butter) may require considerable standing time, while thin, brittle ones may need almost none. (Where it's necessary to work very fast, we've noted this right in the recipe.) In any case, it is important not to dally when the cookies are ready, as they will continue to bake until removed from the cookie sheet and some may become rigid and stuck. Whenever cookies have inadvertently cooled and hardened, instead of prying them up and risking breakage, return the baking sheet to the oven for a few minutes to soften them again.

Cookie sheets should also be cooled completely between batches to keep the dough from warming too much, which can cause the cookies to flatten and spread and in some cases can even cause the butter in the cookies to melt. To avoid any problems, have a couple of extra cookie sheets on hand and rotate among them.

Baking Cookies at High Altitudes

In general, up to 3,000 feet, no adjustments are necessary to obtain attractive, properly textured cookies. When baking above 3,000 feet, reduce the oven temperature by about 25 degrees, which helps the cookies retain moisture. It also helps to reduce the sugar in the recipe by 2 tablespoons for every 1 cup. For rich chocolaty or very sweet

doughs, slightly reducing the baking powder may be helpful. Above 5,000 feet, it is sometimes necessary to reduce baking powder by half and sugar by about 2 tablespoons for every cup. In sour cream doughs, the baking soda should not be reduced beyond ½ teaspoon for every cup of sour cream.

Decorating Cookies

We've always liked the idea of decorations that provide a clue to a cookie's flavor: a sprinkling of cinnamon and sugar to advertise a hint of spices; a few coconut shreds to signal a coconut filling. Coarsely chopped nuts or chocolate chips are wonderful toppings for big, flavorful, rough-textured cookies, but would be out of place on delicate wafers and crisps. Likewise, fine piping, tiny nonpareils, crystal sugar, or dainty dabs of jam are fine for tea cookies, but would seem fussy on hefty drop cookies and bars. Don't overdo it, though. A good general rule is to keep cookie decorations simple.

Quick Cookie Icing

About 1 cup

This is good for children's cookie making. It can be tinted with food coloring and spread on gingerbread or sugar cookies. Mix up a thick batch for piping out of sealable plastic bags (cut off one bottom corner).

In a medium bowl, stir together until smooth:

4 cups powdered sugar
3 to 4 tablespoons water
Adjust the consistency as necessary with more:
Powdered sugar or water
Color as desired. To store, cover the surface of the icing with a sheet of plastic wrap.

> ### QUICK LEMON ICING FOR COOKIES
>
> *Perfect on Iced Sugar Cookies, 60. Prepare Quick Cookie Icing, left, substituting fresh lemon juice for the water.*

Royal Icing with Fresh Egg White

About 6 tablespoons

This decorative icing dries hard like plaster and is pure white unless tinted with food coloring. Made with a bit less sugar, it is spreadable (or you can add a little water); otherwise, it is stiff enough to pipe and makes beautiful filigree, lace, tiny dots, and string work. Royal Icing is mostly sugar and not especially delicious. Our advice is to use it only when decoration is more important than taste or in very small quantities. Royal Icing is usually made by beating powdered sugar into raw egg whites. In our version, the egg whites are heated to 160°F as a safeguard against salmonella bacteria.

In a microwave-safe bowl, stir together until thoroughly combined:
1 large egg white
⅔ cup powdered sugar
Microwave on high until the mixture reaches 160°F on an instant-read thermometer (it should not exceed 175°F), 30 to 60 seconds. If you need to take more than one temperature reading, wash the thermometer thoroughly or dip it into a mug of boiling water before taking additional readings. Add and beat on high speed until the icing is cool and holds stiff peaks:
⅔ cup powdered sugar
If the icing is not stiff enough, add more:
Powdered sugar
Color, if desired, with liquid or powdered food coloring (the color will intensify as the icing stands). The icing can be stored in a covered container for up to 3 days. Cover the surface of the icing with a piece of wax paper or parchment paper to prevent drying. The icing can be rebeaten if necessary. To pipe, use a small pastry bag fitted with a fine tip, or cut off the corner of a sealable plastic bag or the tip of a parchment paper cone.

> ### ROYAL ICING WITH POWDERED EGG WHITE
>
> Beat together until stiff peaks form:
> 1⅓ cups powdered sugar
> 1 tablespoon powdered egg white
> 2 tablespoons water
> Color if desired with liquid or powdered food coloring. Use and store as directed above. Tightly covered, this keeps for up to 2 weeks.

Translucent Sugar Glaze

About ½ cup

This glaze gives any plain cookie a slightly shiny crust and a bit of extra sweetness. Double the recipe for a large batch of cookies.

Stir together briskly until thoroughly combined:

1 cup powdered sugar, sifted if lumpy

2 to 3 tablespoons water, liquor, fresh lemon juice, or coffee
½ teaspoon grated orange or lemon zest (optional)
¼ teaspoon vanilla (optional)

Brush or use a spoon to drizzle over the cookies. Do not store.

Honey Glaze

About ¼ cup

Spread or brush on cookies.

Combine in a small saucepan and bring to a boil:

¼ cup honey
2 tablespoons sugar
1 tablespoon unsalted butter

This keeps, refrigerated, for about 3 weeks. Reheat before using.

HOW TO DECORATE COOKIES

Decorations greatly assist the appearance (and disappearance) of cookies. A number of different techniques can be employed, just about all of which are suited to small hands.

1 Nonpareils are perhaps the simplest of cookie decorations. To ensure that nonpareils and other garnishes will stay on top of cookies, press them firmly into the dough before baking (use a wide-bladed spatula if the cookies are flat). Or secure them after baking with *Royal Icing, 12.*

2 Cookies can also be decorated with food-coloring paint. To paint cookies before baking, whisk together an egg yolk, about ¼ teaspoon water, and a drop of the desired food coloring. (Remember that blue coloring will turn green when mixed with the yellow yolk; for a true blue, use egg white instead.)

For paint to be applied after baking, simply combine a drop of food coloring with a bit of water to dilute it to the appropriate intensity. (Keep in mind that this color wash shows up well only on Springerle, sugar cookies, and other light-colored cookies.) Apply the paint in either case with a soft, fine-tipped paintbrush—or a small pastry brush if detail isn't important.

3 Or you could choose to pipe filigree or write script using a paper cone made of wax or parchment paper (opposite). The best mixtures for fine piping are *Royal Icing, 12,* and plain melted chocolate (thinned if necessary with drops of flavorless vegetable oil).

4 Or use a small sealable plastic bag for piping. Once it is filled with icing, gather up and twist the plastic bag, forcing the frosting toward a bottom corner. Snip the end to make a tiny opening for piping. Test the size of the opening by practicing on a plate; snip the opening larger if necessary.

HOW TO MAKE A PAPER CONE

You can use a paper cone instead of a pastry bag to pipe icing onto cookies. Paper cones are especially effective for use with small amounts of icing or with icing in a number of different colors. Start by snipping a small bit off the tip of the cone for piping. Test the size of the opening by practicing piping on a plate; snip a larger opening if a thicker line of icing is desired.

1 Start with a piece of parchment paper that measures 15 inches long by 11 inches wide. Keeping one of the long sides in front of you, fold the paper diagonally in half.

2 Keeping your index finger in the center of the fold, begin shaping the cone by holding the paper at one end of the fold and rolling it toward the center. The point of the cone will form in the center of the fold.

3 Continue rolling the cone, keeping its point as tight as possible. Use your fingers to guide and secure the point.

4 Adjust the tightness at the point of the cone by pulling on the ends of the paper.

5 Fold down the shorter ends of the paper to secure the shape and size of the cone before filling it with icing.

6 Once the cone is filled with icing, fold the ends of the paper toward the point to keep the icing from leaking out. Snip a small bit of the tip off the end of the cone and begin piping.

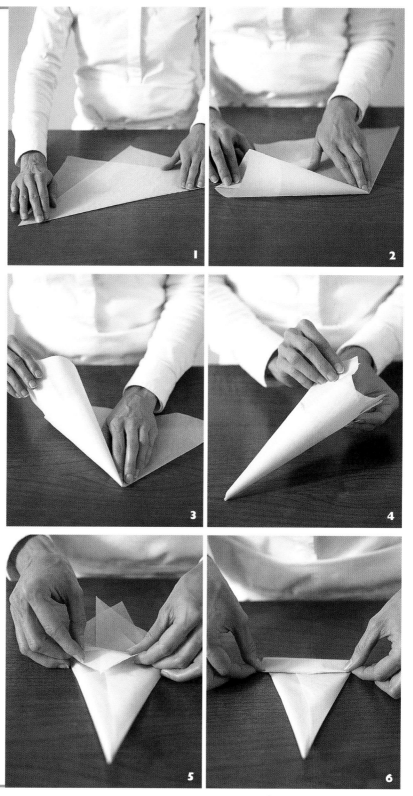

Storing Cookies

Packaging: Plastic storage containers and sealable plastic bags keep cookies airtight. Still, as long as their lids fit tightly, old-fashioned cookie tins do the job nicely and have a lot more charm. Never store cookies in any kind of container until they have completely cooled. Warm cookies will produce steam, which will cause the entire batch to soften, and eventually to spoil. If cookies have been iced or painted, let the icing or coloring set up and dry completely before storing them.

Separating flavors: Cookies can generally be stored at room temperature for 1 to 2 weeks. Pack each type of cookie in a separate container. Otherwise, butter cookies and mild bars will quickly take on the flavors of the spicy, citrusy kinds, and snaps and crisps will go soft from moisture borrowed from thicker, chunkier ones. For extra-large cookies and oversized bars, store individually in small sealable plastic bags.

Freezing: Although cookies have a well-deserved reputation for keeping better than other baked desserts, most are truly at their peak of flavor in the first few days. Even with cookies that benefit from some mellowing, like the spicy honey kinds, fresh flavors begin to fade after several weeks. And cookies laden with butter and nuts may develop off-flavors as the butterfat and the oil in the nuts go stale. Fortunately, most cookie varieties freeze well, staying moist and retaining their just-baked flavor for a month if packed in airtight containers. Brownies, chocolate chip and sugar cookies, and thin, crispy varieties freeze particularly well. If freezing bar cookies, pack them away uncut, then cut into servings when partially thawed. Cookies that are sprinkled with or rolled in sugar, or that are to be frosted or glazed, should be frozen without these enhancements. Allow them to defrost completely before sugar coating, glazing, or frosting.

If you want to eat frozen cookies right away, lay them on baking sheets and warm in a preheated 300°F oven for a few minutes. Homemade, or even store-bought, cookies that have gone limp from exposure to humidity can also be rejuvenated and crisped this way. When setting cookies out to thaw, it is best to leave them partially unwrapped so they can breathe and condensation doesn't build up.

Packaging Cookies for Shipping and Gift Giving

The best choices are small and medium cookies, at least ¼ inch thick and firm in consistency, although softer brownies, blondies, and other bar cookies also usually ship well—with the exception of bars with sticky fillings or icings. (Cut bar cookies into portions and wrap individually in plastic wrap, then pack in airtight containers before shipping.)

More delicate varieties can also be mailed successfully if they are packed carefully in tins or tough plastic boxes with plenty of crumpled wax or parchment paper added to keep them from jostling each other. Extremely thin, brittle cookies and tender, crumbly ones do not travel well, nor do cookies with sticky glazes or with moist fillings such as jam or buttercream. Chewy-soft or fragile meringue kisses and other egg white cookies are likewise an unwise choice; in fact, they may disintegrate completely if thrown about.

After cookies are placed in durable rigid containers, they then need to be packed in larger boxes filled with Styrofoam bits, plastic bubble sheets, crumpled newspaper, or other airy filler to cushion the goodies inside from bumps and knocks. As added insurance that the cookies will arrive at their destination unbroken, consider shipping them by air.

Pretty metal cookie tins, ceramic cookie jars, clear glass storage jars, and decorative wooden boxes all make a gift of home-baked cookies more special. Secure containers with loose lids by tying them up with a beautiful ribbon. If you have a modicum of sewing ability, you can also present cookies in fabric sacks tied with ribbon or fancy twist-ties made with wire ribbon. (Slip a plastic bag, cut down to size if necessary, inside the fabric for an airtight liner.) Small, dainty cookies can also be tucked in colored bonbon papers or mini-cupcake cups in flat candy boxes. For a special touch, tie a ribbon around the gift bag or box and secure a cookie cutter in the bow.

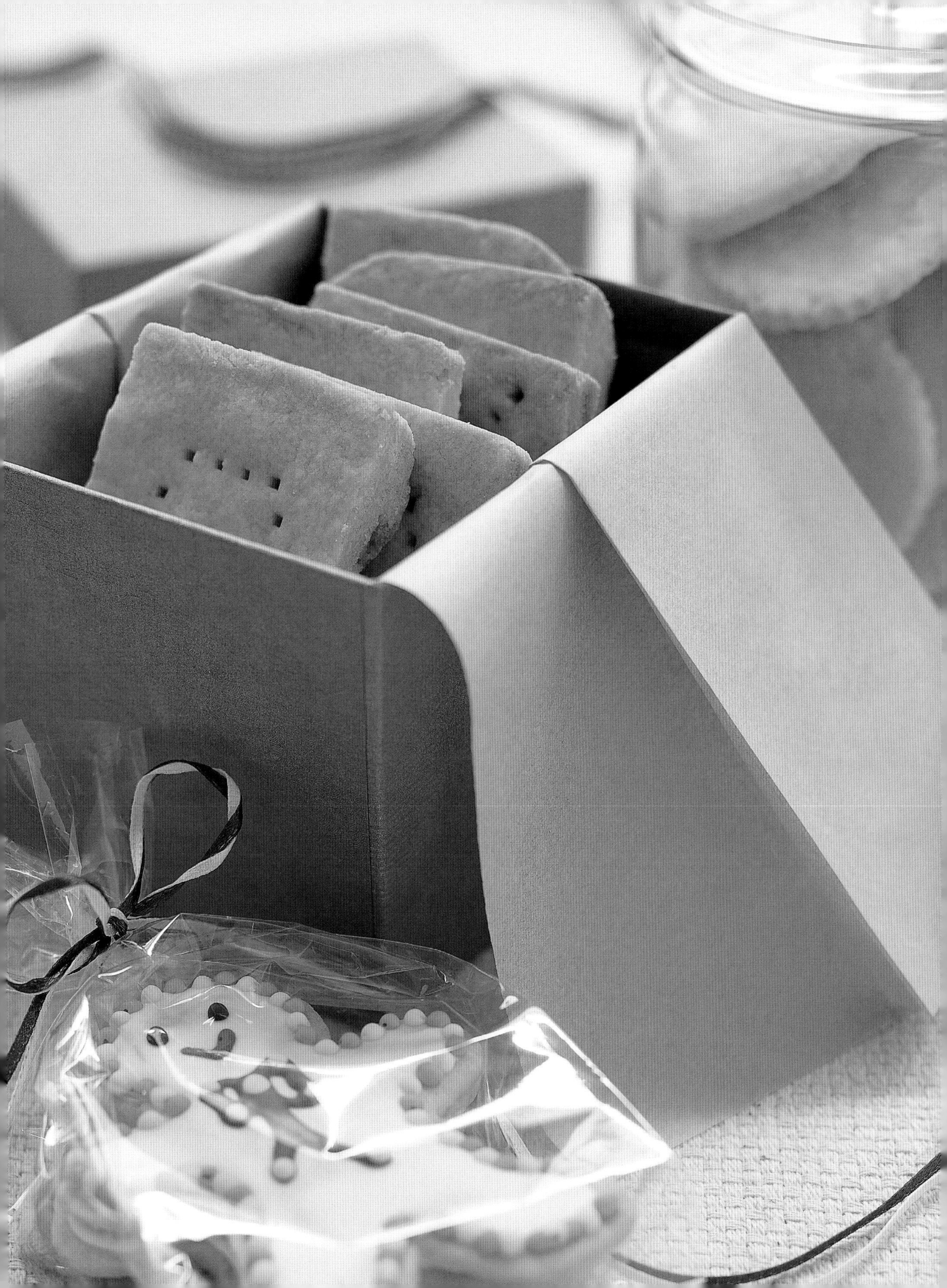

Cookie Menus

CHILDREN'S CHRISTMAS PARTY
Iced Sugar Cookies, 60
Gingerbread People, 67
Almond Thumbprint Cookies, 99

HOLIDAY OPEN HOUSE
Rich Rolled Sugar Cookies, 64
Brandied Fruitcake Drops, 95
Pecan Tassies, 101
Austrian Wreaths (**1**), 100
Mandelbrezeln, 86

HOLIDAY GIFT GIVING
Dream Bars, 49
Coconut Macaroons, 30
Florentines Cockaigne, 32
Viennese Crescents, 82
Ginger Snaps, 77
Bourbon Balls, 95

EUROPEAN CHRISTMAS TRADITION
Mother Kroll's Lebkuchen, 55
Cinnamon Stars, 70
Pfeffernüsse, 83
Drei Augen, 98
Spritz Cookies, 123
Springerle (**2**), 124
Spekulatius, 121

COOKIE CARE PACKAGE
Brownies Cockaigne, 40
Candy Bar Bars, 52
Peanut Butter Chocolate Chunk
    Monsters, 27
Classic Peanut Butter Cookies, 74

MORNING COFFEE
Classic Oatmeal Cookies, 24
Rugelach, 105
Lemon Poppy Seed Cookies, 63

TEA PARTY
Lemon Curd Bars Cockaigne, 46
Scottish Shortbread, 57
Cranberry Cherry Pinwheels, 106

VALENTINE'S DAY
Petticoat Tails, 57
Glazed Lemon Dainties, 93
Raspberry Streusel Bars, 48
Linzer Hearts, 98

HALLOWEEN PARTY
Raisin-Spice Cookies, 63
Spiced Apple Bars, 46
Snickerdoodles, 75

BABY SHOWER
Meringue Nut Kisses, 28
Gram Mencke's Fudge Drops, 36
Benne Seed Wafers, 85

MOTHER'S DAY
Madeleines (**3**), 120
Marble Cookies, 63
Raspberry Streusel Bars, 48

THANK-YOU GIFT
Classic Chocolate Chip Cookies, 22
Sablés, 68
Chocolate-Coated Mocha Biscotti, 89

WEDDING SHOWER
Almond Macaroons, 30
Pecan Lace, 34
Mexican Wedding Cakes, 81
Lemon Butter Cookies, 63
Kourambiedes, 85

AFTER DINNER TREATS
Tuiles, 35
Cantuccini, 87
Chocolate Mint Surprises, 103
Cornmeal Citrus Cookies, 63
Palm Leaves, 90

BOOK CLUB MEETING
Blondies, 41
Classic Biscotti, 88
Mocha Java Congo Bars, 52
Orange Ginger Wafers, 77

DIET BEGINS TOMORROW
Cheesecake Brownies, 45
White Chocolate Macadamia
    Monsters, 27
Chocolate-Glazed Toffee Bars (**4**), 50

ESPECIALLY FOR CHRISTMAS
We have placed a snowflake symbol ❄ next to the recipes for cookies traditionally made during the holiday season.

ABOUT
DROP
COOKIES

*E*xcept for bars, drop cookies are the easiest cookies to make, because shaping usually involves nothing more than dropping dough from a spoon. A few recipes call for patting down the dough or spreading it out with the tip of a knife. In most cases, drop cookies are very forgiving: If the mixture is slightly stiffer or softer than expected, no harm is done; the results will just be a little flatter or puffier than usual.

Occasionally, however, when the batter must be very fluid, as with Pecan Lace, 34, the consistency has to be just right for the desired amount of spreading. When working with this kind of batter, you may want to test bake a cookie or two. If the finished cookie is too thick or has spread too much during baking, stir in a little liquid or flour to thin or stiffen the mixture.

The recipes call for dropping dough or batter from a measuring teaspoon or tablespoon. This is for the sake of precision and helps ensure that recipe yields and baking times are accurate.

Classic Chocolate Chip Cookies, 22

Classic Chocolate Chip Cookies

About 3 dozen 2½-inch cookies

Chocolate chips come in various flavors and sizes and are formulated to withstand normal oven heat and to hold their shape in baked desserts without melting, even though the fat is fully melted. For that reason, they should not be substituted for bar chocolates in recipes that require melted chocolate.

Position a rack in the center of the oven. Preheat the oven to 375°F. Grease cookie sheets. Whisk together thoroughly:

**1 cup plus 2 tablespoons
all-purpose flour**
½ teaspoon baking soda

Beat on medium speed until very fluffy and well blended:

**8 tablespoons (1 stick) unsalted
butter, softened**
½ cup sugar
½ cup packed light brown sugar

Add and beat on medium speed until well combined:

1 large egg
¼ teaspoon salt
1½ teaspoons vanilla

Stir the flour mixture into the butter mixture until well blended and smooth. Stir in:

1 cup semisweet chocolate chips

**¾ cup chopped walnuts or pecans
(optional)**

Drop the dough by heaping measuring teaspoonfuls onto the sheets, spacing about 2 inches apart. Bake, 1 sheet at a time, until the cookies are just slightly colored on top and rimmed with brown at the edges, 8 to 10 minutes; rotate the sheet halfway through baking for even browning. Remove the sheet to a rack and let stand until the cookies firm slightly, about 2 minutes. Transfer the cookies to racks to cool.

VANILLA

The long, thin vanilla bean is a pod from the orchid flower of a tropical vine and has no flavor when picked. In curing for several months, tiny fragrant white crystals called vanillin are secreted from the pod's lining. The pod wrinkles a bit and turns chocolate brown. **Pure vanilla extract** is prepared by steeping the cured pods in alcohol.

Oatmeal Chocolate Chip Cookies (Reduced Fat)

About 3 dozen 2½- to 2¾-inch cookies

These cookies have 3.3 grams of fat apiece. This recipe was developed to give chocolate chip cookie lovers a lean alternative.

Position a rack in the center of the oven. Preheat the oven to 375°F. Coat cookie sheets with nonstick spray.

Whisk together thoroughly:

1¼ cups all-purpose flour
¾ teaspoon baking soda
¾ teaspoon baking powder
¼ teaspoon salt

Beat on medium speed until well blended:

¼ cup corn or canola oil
**2 tablespoons unsalted butter,
softened**
1 cup packed dark brown sugar
1 large egg
1 large egg white
⅓ cup light or dark corn syrup

1 tablespoon skim milk
2½ teaspoons vanilla

Stir into the batter:

2 cups old-fashioned rolled oats
**1 cup reduced-fat semisweet
chocolate chips**

Let the mixture stand for 10 minutes so the oats can absorb some moisture. Stir in the flour mixture; the dough will be slightly soft. Drop the dough by heaping measuring tablespoonfuls onto the sheets, spacing about 2½ inches apart.

Bake, 1 sheet at a time, until the cookies are tinged with brown all over and the centers are just barely firm when lightly pressed, 7 to 10 minutes; be careful not to overbake. Remove the sheet to a rack and let stand until the cookies firm slightly, about 2 minutes. Transfer the cookies to racks to cool.

HOW TO BEAT (CREAM) THE BUTTER AND SUGAR UNTIL LIGHT

This is the essential first step in mixing many doughs: beating butter and sugar together until the mixture appears lighter in color and texture because of the incorporation of air. Well-creamed butter and sugar creates the initial structure of the dough, enabling the addition of other ingredients without causing that structure to collapse. Start with butter at 65° to 70°F (butter should be firm but malleable, not soft and squishy) for the proper friction necessary to beat air into the mixture without overly softening or melting it.

1 To cream butter and sugar by hand, begin mashing the butter against the side of the bowl with a wooden spoon. Scrape the mass together as necessary and repeat the mashing motion until the butter is softened.

2 Add the sugar gradually and work the butter and sugar together until the mixture is light in color and texture. It will look like sugary frosting. If it is curdled or frothy, you have worked it too long and the oil in the butter has separated. The result will be a coarse-grained cookie. Correct the situation by refrigerating the mixture for 5 to 10 minutes before continuing to beat.

3 and 4 To cream butter and sugar by machine, beat the butter at low speed for about 30 seconds until it is creamy. Add the sugar gradually and, if using a handheld mixer, beat at high speed until the mixture is light in color and texture and resembles a sugary frosting. This usually requires from 3 to 7 minutes, depending on quantities. If using a heavy-duty mixer that offers a choice between a whisk and paddle, use the paddle and beat on medium speed for less time. If the mixture looks curdled or begins to ooze melted butter, you have mixed too long, or your ingredients were too warm. Correct the situation by refrigerating the mixture for 5 to 10 minutes before continuing to beat.

Classic Oatmeal Cookies

About 3½ dozen 3-inch cookies

These are homey and nubby-textured and have a mild brown sugar and oats flavor.

Position a rack in the upper third of the oven. Preheat the oven to 350°F. Grease cookie sheets.

Whisk together thoroughly:

1¾ cups all-purpose flour
¾ teaspoon baking soda
¾ teaspoon baking powder
½ teaspoon salt
½ teaspoon ground cinnamon
½ teaspoon ground nutmeg

Beat on medium speed until well blended:

½ pound (2 sticks) unsalted butter, softened
1½ cups packed light or dark brown sugar
¼ cup sugar
2 large eggs
2½ teaspoons vanilla

Stir the flour mixture into the butter mixture until well blended and smooth. Stir in:

1 cup raisins, chopped
3½ cups old-fashioned rolled oats

Drop the dough by heaping measuring tablespoonfuls onto the sheets, spacing about 3 inches apart. With lightly greased hands, lightly press the cookies down to form ½-inch-thick rounds. (If necessary, wipe off your hands and regrease to prevent the dough from sticking to them.) Bake, 1 sheet at a time, until the cookies are lightly browned all over and almost firm when lightly pressed in the center of the top, 6 to 9 minutes; rotate the sheet halfway through baking for even browning. Remove the sheet to a rack and let stand until the cookies firm slightly, about 2 minutes. Transfer the cookies to racks to cool.

CINNAMON, NUTMEG, AND MACE

True cinnamon is the bark of a tree that flourishes in Ceylon and along the Malabar Coast. It is extremely mild, whether rolled in a tight quill or stick or in powdered form.

Two spices come from the brown, oval seed of a fruit resembling an apricot, which grows on a tropical evergreen tree. Wrapped around the shell of the seed is a lacy sheath, which is ground before packing. A blade of mace is one segment of the lacy covering, called the aril. Scarlet when the fruit is opened, the aril dries to a shade of orange. Several weeks after harvest, when the kernel has shrunk in its shell, the thin shell is cracked and the kernel removed. This is nutmeg—brown, solid, and hard. Nutmeg is best freshly grated. As warm a spice as nutmeg is, mace is more refined and can be used in place of nutmeg.

Hermits

About 4½ dozen 2½-inch cookies

For best flavor, let these cookies mellow a few hours before serving.

Position a rack in the upper third of the oven. Preheat the oven to 375°F. Grease cookie sheets.

Stir together:

1 cup raisins
1 cup chopped dates
¾ cup chopped walnuts
3 tablespoons hot water

Whisk together thoroughly:

2⅔ cups all-purpose flour
1 teaspoon baking powder
¾ teaspoon baking soda
¼ teaspoon salt
2¼ teaspoons ground cinnamon
½ teaspoon ground cloves
¼ teaspoon ground nutmeg

Beat on medium speed until very fluffy and well blended:

½ pound (2 sticks) unsalted butter, softened
1 cup packed light brown sugar
⅔ cup sugar

Add and beat until well combined:

2 large eggs
2½ tablespoons milk
2½ teaspoons vanilla
½ teaspoon finely grated orange zest

Stir half of the flour mixture into the butter mixture until well blended and smooth. Stir in the raisin mixture, followed by the remaining flour mixture, until well blended. Drop the dough by heaping measuring tablespoonfuls onto the sheets, spacing about 1½ inches apart. Bake, 1 sheet at a time, until the cookies are tinged with brown all over and slightly darker at the edges, 9 to 12 minutes. Remove the sheet to a rack and let stand until the cookies firm slightly, about 2 minutes. Transfer the cookies to racks to cool.

Oatmeal Raisin Monsters

About twelve 4-inch or fifty 2½-inch cookies

This is a particularly tasty version of an indispensable classic. Oatmeal cookies are best made with either all granulated or all brown sugar. Granulated sugar will give you crispier cookies, while the molasses in brown sugar yields a moister cookie with a richer flavor.

Position a rack in the center of the oven. Preheat the oven to 325°F. Grease cookie sheets or cover with parchment paper or greased aluminum foil.

Beat on medium speed until very fluffy and well blended:

½ pound (2 sticks) unsalted butter, softened

1⅓ cups sugar

Beat in 1 at a time until well combined:

2 large eggs

Add:

1 teaspoon vanilla

Mix in until just combined:

2 cups old-fashioned rolled oats

2 cups all-purpose flour

1 teaspoon baking soda

⅛ teaspoon salt

Add and stir to mix:

1⅓ cups raisins

Using ⅓ cup for each monster, drop the dough onto the sheets, spacing about 3 inches apart. Bake, 1 sheet at a time, until the cookies are golden brown, 20 to 25 minutes. For regular-sized cookies, drop by heaping measuring teaspoonfuls 1½ inches apart and bake for 15 minutes. Remove the sheet to a rack and let stand until the cookies firm slightly. Transfer the cookies to racks to cool.

Peanut Butter Chocolate Chunk Monsters

About sixteen 4-inch or fifty 2½-inch cookies

Position a rack in the center of the oven. Preheat the oven to 350°F. Grease cookie sheets or cover with parchment paper or greased aluminum foil.
Beat on medium speed until very fluffy and well blended:

14 tablespoons (1¾ sticks) unsalted butter, softened

2 cups sugar

½ cup packed dark brown sugar

Beat in 1 at a time until well combined:

3 large eggs

Mix in:

1½ cups creamy peanut butter

¾ teaspoon vanilla

Stir in until just combined:

2¼ cups all-purpose flour

¾ teaspoon baking soda

¼ teaspoon salt

Add and stir until mixed:

1 cup coarsely chopped bittersweet or semisweet chocolate

¾ cup unsalted shelled peanuts

Using ⅓ cup for each monster, drop the dough onto the sheets, spacing about 3 inches apart. Bake, 1 sheet at a time, until the cookies are golden brown, 20 to 25 minutes. For regular-sized cookies, drop by heaping measuring teaspoonfuls 1½ inches apart and bake for 20 minutes. Remove the sheet to a rack and let stand until the cookies firm slightly. Transfer the cookies to racks to cool.

White Chocolate Macadamia Monsters

About fourteen 4½-inch or forty 3-inch cookies

Position a rack in the center of the oven. Preheat the oven to 325°F. Grease cookie sheets or cover with parchment paper or greased aluminum foil.
Beat on medium speed until very fluffy and well blended:

20 tablespoons (2½ sticks) unsalted butter, softened

1⅓ cups sugar

⅔ cup packed dark brown sugar

Beat in 1 at a time:

2 large eggs

Stir in:

½ teaspoon vanilla

Stir in just until combined:

2½ cups all-purpose flour

1 teaspoon baking soda

⅛ teaspoon salt

Stir in:

1 cup macadamia nuts

1 cup coarsely chopped white chocolate

Using ⅓ cup for each monster, drop the dough onto the sheets, spacing about 3 inches apart. Bake, 1 sheet at a time, until the cookies are golden brown, 20 to 25 minutes. For regular-sized cookies, drop by heaping measuring teaspoonfuls 1½ inches apart and bake for 15 to 17 minutes. Remove the sheet to a rack and let stand until the cookies firm slightly. Transfer the cookies to racks to cool.

WHITE CHOCOLATE

White chocolate resembles milk chocolate in composition except that it contains no chocolate liquor, which is why it is ivory, not brown. The cocoa butter it contains gives it a very mild, milk-chocolate flavor and a creamy mouth feel. This product should not be confused with white confectionery coating, which is made with a vegetable fat other than cocoa butter. White chocolate is used most frequently in cheesecakes, light-textured cakes, mousses, and icings when a delicate chocolate flavor is desired.

Meringue Nut Kisses (Reduced Fat)

About 3 dozen 1½-inch cookies

Although normally we advise against putting 2 cookie sheets in the oven at once, meringues bake in a very low oven and brown only slightly—so you can bake 2 sheets at the same time.

Have all ingredients at room temperature, 68° to 70°F. Position a rack in the center of the oven and another in the upper third. Preheat the oven to 250°F. Cover cookie sheets with parchment paper.

In a medium bowl, beat on low speed until foamy:

4 large egg whites
⅛ teaspoon salt
⅛ teaspoon fresh lemon juice

Increase the speed to high and beat until the egg whites are frothy and just begin to form soft peaks. Gradually add and beat until well combined, scraping the sides of the bowl as necessary:

1 cup sugar

Reduce the speed to low and add:

2 teaspoons vanilla
½ teaspoon almond extract (omit if pecans are used)

Beat until the mixture is glossy and stands in very stiff peaks. Fold in:

½ cup finely chopped pecans, almonds, or skinned hazelnuts

Using a heaping measuring teaspoonful for each cookie, drop the batter onto the sheets in peaked mounds, spacing about 1½ inches apart. (Alternatively, pipe the batter into 1¼-inch kisses using a pastry bag fitted with a ½-inch-diameter open star tip.)

Bake, 2 sheets at a time, for 18 minutes. Rotate the sheets and switch racks. Bake for 18 minutes more. Turn the heat off and let the cookies stand in the oven for 30 minutes. With the cookies still attached to the paper, place on a flat surface until completely cool. Gently peel the cookies from the paper.

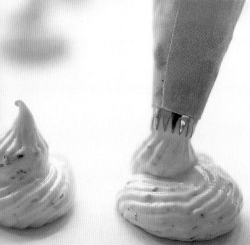

Coconut Almond Macaroons

About 5 dozen 1¾-inch cookies

These cookies are crispy outside and moist and chewy inside.

Position a rack in the center of the oven. Preheat the oven to 350°F. Cover cookie sheets with parchment paper or greased aluminum foil. Beat until they hold soft peaks:

4 large egg whites

Gradually add, a few tablespoons at a time:

1⅓ cups sugar

Combine:

¾ cup blanched almonds, finely ground

1 cup flaked or shredded sweetened coconut

Gently fold this mixture into the beaten egg whites. Drop the dough by measuring tablespoonfuls onto the sheets, spacing about 2 inches apart. Bake, 1 sheet at a time, until the cookies are lightly golden, for 20 minutes. Remove the sheet to a rack and let stand until the cookies are slightly cool. Carefully peel the cookies from the paper or foil and transfer to racks until completely cool.

HOW TO BEAT AND FOLD EGG WHITES

Egg whites can increase in volume by as much as nine times when beaten correctly, so choose a bowl large and deep enough. Avoid plastic bowls and always be sure that bowl, beater, and scraper are absolutely free of grease and detergent. If in doubt, wipe with lemon juice or vinegar, rinse, and dry carefully. Beaten egg whites do not hold up well, so start beating only when all other ingredients are mixed and ready. If the beaten egg whites are headed for the oven, have the oven preheated.

Egg whites can be beaten by hand or with an electric mixer. Do not use a blender or food processor. If beating by hand, be prepared to give your forearm a workout—about 300 strokes in 2 minutes for 2 egg whites.

The key to a successful egg foam is to stop beating when the eggs are stiff but not dry. Overbeating causes the whites to turn grainy and brittle, making it difficult to incorporate them into a batter without rupturing the air cells. To determine if the whites are beaten sufficiently, some cooks use the inverted bowl test: the whites should cling tenaciously to the bottom of the upside-down bowl. A less risky method is to lift your whisk or beater to check the condition of the peaks of the egg whites; the foam should be just stiff enough to stand up in well-defined, unwavering peaks. In the making of meringues and some cakes, sugar is beaten into the egg whites when they have reached the soft-peak stage. Add the sugar gradually to ensure that it will dissolve. Although sugar reduces volume slightly, it produces a sturdier foam.

1 Using a thin-wired, flexible whisk, begin slowly and lightly with a very relaxed wrist motion and beat steadily until the egg whites lose their translucency and become foamy.

2 At this point, gradually increase the beating tempo, using large hand motions to incorporate the maximum air, and continue without stopping until the whites are airy and have reached the desired stage of firmness.

Follow the same principle with an electric mixer, starting on low speed and increasing speed as the whites become foamy and then begin to stiffen. When working with a hand-held mixer, push the beaters around the bowl, moving them up and *through* the whites to incorporate more air and similarly starting on low speed and progressing to high.

3 To fold beaten egg whites into a batter, use a large rubber spatula to scoop about one-quarter of the egg whites onto the top of the batter. Use the edge of the spatula to cut through the middle of the egg whites down to the bottom of the bowl. Draw the spatula toward you, scraping a big scoop of batter up the side of the bowl, and lift and turn the spatula so that the batter falls gently back on top of the egg whites in the center. Rotate the bowl slightly and repeat the steps, always cutting into the center of the biggest mass of egg whites as you proceed. When these first egg whites are well incorporated, scrape all of the remaining egg whites on top of the batter and fold them in as described.

Almond Macaroons

About 2½ dozen 1¾-inch cookies

Have all ingredients at room temperature, 68° to 70°F. Position 2 racks in the center of the oven. Preheat the oven to 350°F. Cover cookie sheets with parchment paper or well-greased aluminum foil.

Combine in a food processor and process until finely chopped, scraping the sides of the bowl as necessary:

7 ounces almond paste, cut into small pieces
1 cup powdered sugar

With the machine running, slowly pour through the feed tube and process until the mixture is smooth, about 1 minute:

3 large egg whites
¼ teaspoon almond extract (optional)

Transfer the mixture to a large, heavy saucepan. Cook, stirring constantly, over medium heat until slightly thickened, about 4 minutes. Refrigerate until cooled and slightly firm.

Drop by heaping measuring teaspoonfuls onto the sheets, spacing about 2 inches apart. Bake, 2 sheets at a time, just until the cookies are tinged with brown but still soft inside, 19 to 24 minutes; rotate the sheets halfway through baking for even browning. Remove the sheets to racks and let stand until the cookies cool. Carefully peel the cookies from the paper or foil and transfer to racks to dry out.

Chocolate Almond Macaroons

About 8 dozen 1¼-inch cookies

A dark, crispy, and rugged-looking exterior hides a chewy center packed with coconut, almonds, and chocolate.

Position a rack in the center of the oven. Preheat the oven to 350°F. Cover cookie sheets with parchment paper or greased aluminum foil.

Combine and set aside:

1⅔ cups blanched almonds, finely ground
2 cups plus 2 tablespoons flaked or shredded sweetened coconut

Melt, stirring often, in the top of a double boiler or in a microwave on medium:

3 ounces bittersweet or semisweet chocolate

Cool to room temperature.
Beat until they hold soft peaks:

3 large egg whites

Gradually add, a few tablespoons at a time:

1 cup sugar

Continue beating until the mixture is very stiff and glossy. Fold the nut mixture into the beaten egg whites, alternating with the melted chocolate, beginning and ending with the nut mixture. Drop by measuring teaspoonfuls onto the sheets, spacing about 1 inch apart. Bake, 1 sheet at a time, until the cookies are lightly browned, for 15 minutes. Remove the sheet to a rack and let stand until the cookies are slightly cool. Carefully peel the cookies from the paper or foil and transfer to racks until completely cool.

Coconut Macaroons

About 2 dozen 1½-inch cookies

All macaroons used to be based on almonds, but the coconut version has been popular for many decades.

Position a rack in the upper third of the oven. Preheat the oven to 325°F. Cover cookie sheets with parchment paper or well-greased aluminum foil.

Stir together until well combined:

⅔ cup sweetened condensed milk
1 large egg white
1½ teaspoons vanilla
⅛ teaspoon salt

Stir in until well blended:

3½ cups flaked or shredded sweetened coconut

Drop the dough by scant measuring tablespoonfuls onto the sheets, spacing about 2 inches apart. Bake, 1 sheet at a time, until the cookies are nicely browned, 20 to 25 minutes. Remove the sheet to a rack and let stand until the cookies are completely cool. Carefully peel the cookies from the paper or foil.

Amaretti (Italian Almond Cookies)

About 4 dozen 2-inch cookies

These delicious little cookies are an-other kind of almond macaroon—a homemade version of the ones sold wrapped in colored tissue paper and packed in red tins.

Position a rack in the center of the oven. Preheat the oven to 300°F. Cover cookie sheets with parchment paper or greased and floured alu-minum foil.

Toast, stirring frequently, in a baking pan until lightly browned, 5 to 8 minutes:

1¾ cups whole natural (unblanched) almonds

Set aside to cool thoroughly. Transfer to a food processor. Add and process until finely ground:

1 cup sugar
2 tablespoons all-purpose flour
⅛ teaspoon salt
Pinch of ground black pepper

Transfer the mixture to a large bowl. Add:

4 large egg whites
1 teaspoon almond extract

½ teaspoon vanilla

Stir a few seconds to combine thor-oughly. Drop by measuring tea-spoonfuls onto the sheets, spacing about 1 inch apart. Bake, 1 sheet at a time, for 25 minutes for chewy cookies or 30 minutes for crisp cookies. Transfer the parchment or foil to a rack and let stand until the cookies are completely cool. With a spatula, gently loosen the cookies from the paper or foil.

Florentines Cockaigne ❄

About 2 dozen 4-inch cookies

A Rombauer family favorite for years, this recipe may be a bit complicated, but it's worth every step. These thin, chewy, candylike Italian cookies are lightly coated on the underside with chocolate. They are particularly popular with those who like the slightly exotic taste of orange, almonds, and chocolate together. Be careful to prepare the chocolate as directed in the recipe, so that it will set up quickly and stay glossy and smooth.

Position a rack in the center of the oven. Preheat the oven to 350°F. Cover 2 cookie sheets with aluminum foil and lightly brush with 1 tablespoon unflavored vegetable oil. Combine in a heavy saucepan:

¾ cup sugar
2 tablespoons honey
⅓ cup heavy cream
8 tablespoons (1 stick) unsalted butter, softened and cut into small pieces

Stir over low heat until the sugar is dissolved, about 5 minutes. Bring to a boil over medium heat, then brush down the sides of the pan with a pastry brush dipped in warm water. Place a warmed candy thermometer in the pan and cook, without stirring, until it reaches the soft-ball stage, 234°F. Remove from the heat and quickly stir in:

1¾ cups finely chopped blanched almonds
¾ cup finely diced candied orange peel or a mixture of candied orange and lemon peel and dried cherries
2 tablespoons all-purpose flour
Finely minced zest of 1 large orange

Drop by measuring tablespoonfuls onto the sheets, spacing about

3 inches apart. Dip the back of a spoon or the tines of a fork into cold water and press the top of each mound to flatten it. Bake, 1 sheet at a time, until the cookies are light golden and set, 8 to 10 minutes; rotate the sheet halfway through baking for even browning. Remove the sheet to a rack and let stand until the cookies are cool. With a small spatula, gently loosen the cookies from the foil.

Melt, stirring often, in the top of a double boiler or in a microwave on medium:

3½ ounces bittersweet or semi-sweet chocolate, very coarsely chopped

Remove from the heat. Add:

1½ ounces bittersweet or semi-sweet chocolate, cut into ½-ounce pieces

Stir until the melted chocolate cools to just barely warm. Remove any unmelted chocolate chunks. Using a table knife or small, thin spatula, immediately spread a thin layer of chocolate over the bottom of each cookie. If the chocolate in the top of the double boiler or bowl starts to set, place it over the bottom of the pan or return it to the microwave for a few seconds and warm just slightly, stirring to blend. Then continue coating the cookies. Let the cookies stand, chocolate side up, until the coating sets completely, about 45 minutes. Store, airtight, in a cool place, between layers of wax paper. These will keep well for up to 10 days. Finished Florentines do not freeze well, but the uncoated cookies may be frozen. To finish, thaw to room temperature and then coat with chocolate.

HOW TO TEST COOKED SUGAR SYRUP

Most experienced cooks use both a thermometer and ice-cold water to test the temperature of cooked sugar syrup. Whether you should let the syrup continue cooking while you are using the ice-cold water test depends on how quickly you work. If testing takes you several minutes, remove the pan from the heat, remembering that doing so cools the syrup and can delay the cooking; if you are an old hand at this, leave the pan on the heat, as a few seconds won't make much difference.

To perform the ice-cold water test, use a clean wooden spoon or a metal spoon (run under hot water to warm it) to drop a small quantity of sugar syrup—less than a teaspoonful—into a small container of very cold (*not* ice) water.

Keeping your fingers submerged, quickly gather the syrup between your fingers. The temperature to which the sugar has been cooked can be identified by the way the syrup reacts. As the water heats and evaporates, the concentration of sugar in the syrup rises; the higher the concentration of sugar, the harder the mixture will be upon cooling.

At 234° to 242°F, a spoonful of syrup dropped into ice-cold water will make a limp, sticky ball that flattens when removed from the water. This is commonly referred to as the soft-ball stage. At 244° to 248°F, the syrup will make a ball that holds its shape and will not flatten when removed from the water. This is called the firm-ball stage. At 250° to 266°F, the syrup will make a hard ball that holds its shape when removed from the water but is still pliable. This is called the hard-ball stage.

Pecan Lace

About 6 dozen 3¼-inch wafers

Since much of the appeal of these see-through wafers is in their brittle, caramelized texture, make them on a dry day.

Have all ingredients at room temperature, 68° to 70°F. Position a rack in the upper third of the oven. Preheat the oven to 350°F. Grease cookie sheets or cover with well-greased aluminum foil.

Toast, stirring constantly, in a baking pan until very lightly browned, 5 to 6 minutes:

½ cup finely chopped pecans

Set aside to cool. Increase the oven temperature to 375°F.

Melt in a medium saucepan over medium heat:

**10 tablespoons (1¼ sticks)
  unsalted butter**

Adjust the heat and boil the butter gently, stirring occasionally, until the solids on the bottom of the pan turn light brown, 3 to 4 minutes.

Remove from the heat and stir in until well blended:

1 cup packed light brown sugar
¼ cup light corn syrup
1 tablespoon milk
¼ teaspoon salt

Stir in until well combined:

1½ cups old-fashioned rolled oats
2 tablespoons all-purpose flour
2 teaspoons vanilla

Stir in the nuts. Drop the batter by scant measuring teaspoonfuls onto the sheets, spacing about 3 inches apart. Don't crowd, as the wafers will spread a great deal. The batter will stiffen as it cools. Bake, 1 sheet at a time, until the cookies are golden brown all over and slightly darker at the edges, 6 to 8 minutes; rotate the sheet halfway through baking for even browning. Remove the sheet to a rack and let stand until the cookies firm slightly, about 1 minute. Gently transfer the cookies to racks to cool. If they become too cool and brittle to be removed easily, return them to the oven for a minute to soften.

Tuiles (French Almond Wafers)

About 2½ dozen 3-inch wafers

These curled wafers are often brought to the table at the end of a special dinner and served with chocolate truffles, coffee, and brandy. Their name is the French word for tiles, because they are shaped like the curved terra-cotta roof tiles so prevalent in the south of France. Almost paper thin, with a subtle almond flavor, tuiles are curled by being draped, while still warm and pliable, over a rolling pin until cool and firm. The step that requires attention is removing them from the baking sheet. The trick is to use a wide spatula with a very thin blade and to work very quickly. Cookie sheets need to be clean and cool before you make a new batch.

Have all ingredients at room temperature, 68° to 70°F. Position a rack in the upper third of the oven. Preheat the oven to 350°F. Very generously grease cookie sheets or cover with parchment paper or well-greased aluminum foil. Have ready several rolling pins or bottles the same width as the rolling pin to shape the wafers.

Warm, stirring constantly, over very low heat until very soft but not thin and runny:

5 tablespoons unsalted butter

Whisk together until very frothy:

2 large egg whites
⅛ teaspoon salt
⅓ cup plus 1 tablespoon sugar
¼ teaspoon almond extract
¼ teaspoon vanilla

Gradually whisk in:

½ cup sifted cake flour (not self-rising)

A bit at a time, whisk in the softened butter until the mixture is well blended and smooth.

Drop the batter by heaping measuring tablespoonfuls onto the sheets, spacing about 3 inches apart. Don't crowd, as the wafers will spread a great deal. Using the tip of a knife and working in a circular motion, spread each portion into a 3-inch round. Very generously sprinkle the rounds with:

½ to ⅔ cup sliced blanched or natural (unblanched) almonds, coarsely chopped

Bake, 1 sheet at a time, until the wafers are rimmed with ½ inch of golden brown, 6 to 9 minutes; rotate the sheet halfway through baking for even browning. Remove the sheet to a rack and let stand for a few seconds. As soon as the wafers can be lifted without tearing, loosen them with a thin-bladed wide metal spatula and slide them, bottom side down, onto rolling pins or bottles. (Remove the wafers to the rolling pins 1 at a time, so the others remain warm and pliable. If some of the wafers cool too quickly to shape on the rolling pins, return the sheet to the oven briefly to warm and soften them.) As soon as the tuiles are firm, transfer to racks to cool.

Brandy Snaps ❄

About 2½ dozen 3-inch-long cookies

Very thin and lacy, these cookies (opposite) are rolled up into cylinders while still warm and filled with whipped cream.

Position a rack in the upper third of the oven. Preheat the oven to 350°F. Cover cookie sheets with well-greased aluminum foil. Have ready 3 or 4 long-handled spoons to use in rolling up the warm wafers. Combine in a medium saucepan and heat, stirring, until the butter is melted but the mixture is not hot:

8 tablespoons (1 stick) unsalted butter
½ cup sugar
⅓ cup light corn syrup or light molasses

Immediately remove from the heat and stir in until smooth:

¾ cup plus 1 tablespoon all-purpose flour
1 teaspoon ground ginger
2 teaspoons brandy
½ teaspoon finely grated lemon or orange zest

Prepare a test cookie by dropping a scant measuring teaspoonful of batter onto a prepared sheet. Bake until bubbly and golden brown, about 7 to 9 minutes. If the cookie does not spread into a wafer-thin layer, thin the batter slightly with a teaspoon or two of water. If the cookie spreads so much it does not hold together, thicken the batter slightly with a tablespoon of all-purpose flour. Once the batter is the correct consistency, drop by scant measuring teaspoonfuls onto the sheets, spacing about 3 inches apart. Don't crowd, as the cookies will spread a great deal. Also, don't bake more than 4 or 5 wafers at a time, as they will cool and firm too rapidly for you to roll them all into cylinders. Bake until the wafers are bubbly and golden brown, 7 to 9 minutes; rotate the sheet halfway through baking for even browning. Immediately remove the sheet to a

rack. As soon as the wafers can be lifted without tearing, loosen them with a thin-bladed wide metal spatula and roll loosely around the spoon handles. (The first several will be very pliable, but the last will have cooled enough to be fairly stiff. If the last ones are too stiff to roll, they can be rewarmed briefly in the oven.) When the cylinders are cool enough to hold their shape, slip them off the handles and let cool completely on racks.

Continue baking and shaping the wafers until all the batter is used. If the batter begins to cool and stiffen during standing, rewarm it slightly over low heat. The foil can be used over and over, but may need to be regreased several times.

Before serving, spoon or pipe into the cylinder ends using a pastry bag fitted with a small open star tip:

Lightly sweetened whipped cream

Serve the brandy snaps immediately.

Gram Mencke's Fudge Drops ❄

About 3 dozen 2½-inch cookies

These cookies were recently given to us by an old family friend who used to cook 20 to 25 varieties of cookies at a time when she got going for the holidays. She remembers that her mother made them, back in the 1920s—so these are no Johnny-come-latelys.

Using an electric mixer, beat until very light:

2 large eggs

Sift together over the eggs and stir to mix:

1 cup sugar
⅔ cup all-purpose flour

1 teaspoon cinnamon
1 teaspoon baking powder
¼ teaspoon salt

Melt, stirring often, in the top of a double boiler or in a microwave on medium:

2 ounces bittersweet or semisweet chocolate

Remove from the heat and add to the egg mixture with:

1 teaspoon vanilla
1 cup chopped walnuts

Stir until well combined. Cover and refrigerate the dough for at least

1 hour or up to 24 hours.

To bake, position a rack in the center of the oven. Preheat the oven to 350°F. Cover cookie sheets with parchment paper or greased aluminum foil.

Drop the dough by heaping measuring teaspoonfuls onto the sheets, spacing about 2 inches apart. Bake, 1 sheet at a time, for 10 to 12 minutes. Transfer the cookies to wire racks to cool.

ABOUT **BAR** COOKIES

*S*ince these are simply spread in a pan, baked, and cut into serv-ing pieces, the time normally taken up with forming dozens of individual cookies is completely eliminated. Still, there can be a lot of variety in bars. They can range from soft-cakey to chewy-gooey to crunchy and brittle. They can also be left plain, or topped with nuts, powdered sugar, or icing; and cut into squares, from very small to very large, or sliced into narrow strips.

When making bar cookies, pay close attention to the size of the pan called for in each recipe. Variations will throw off the baking time and may affect the texture as well. If the pan is too large, the dough may dry out and the bars will be too thin. If the pan is too small, the bars may become gummy in the center or more cakey than they really should be.

Blondies, 41; Brownies Cockaigne, 40

Brownies Cockaigne

Sixteen 3¼ x 2¼-inch or twenty-four 2¼ x 2-inch bars

This recipe has appeared in Joy *since the original 1931 edition.*

Have all ingredients at room temperature, 68° to 70°F. Position a rack in the center of the oven. Preheat the oven to 350°F. Line a 13 x 9-inch baking pan with greased aluminum foil, allowing it to overhang the 2 narrow ends of the pan by about 2 inches.

In a large, heavy saucepan over very low heat, melt, stirring constantly, until the mixture is smooth:

4 ounces unsweetened chocolate, coarsely chopped

8 tablespoons (1 stick) unsalted butter

Set aside to cool completely. Stir in:

2 cups sugar

2 teaspoons vanilla

¼ teaspoon salt

Stir in until well combined:

4 large eggs

Stir in just until combined:

1 cup all-purpose flour

1 cup chopped walnuts or pecans

Scrape the batter into the pan and spread to the edges. Bake until the center is almost firm when lightly pressed and a toothpick inserted in the center comes out clean but still moist at the bottom, 23 to 28 minutes. Remove the pan to a rack and let stand until completely cool. Using the overhanging foil as handles, lift the brownie to a cutting board. Carefully peel off the foil. Cut into bars.

Blondies

Sixteen 2 x 2-inch bars

Position a rack in the center of the oven. Preheat the oven to 350°F. Line an 8 x 8-inch baking pan with greased aluminum foil, allowing it to overhang 2 opposing ends of the pan by about 2 inches.

Toast, stirring occasionally, in a baking pan until very lightly browned, 5 to 8 minutes:

1 cup chopped pecans

Set aside to cool. Whisk together thoroughly:

1 cup all-purpose flour
¼ teaspoon baking powder
⅛ teaspoon baking soda
⅛ teaspoon salt

In a large, heavy saucepan, melt, then boil, stirring constantly, until light golden brown, about 4 minutes:

8 tablespoons (1 stick) unsalted butter

Remove from the heat and stir in until well blended:

⅔ cup packed light brown sugar
¼ cup sugar

Let cool to barely warm. Stir in until well combined:

1 large egg
1 large egg yolk
1 tablespoon light corn syrup
1½ teaspoons vanilla

Stir in the flour mixture and the pecans until well blended. Scrape the batter into the pan and spread to the edges. Bake until the top is golden brown and a toothpick inserted in the thickest part comes out clean, 28 to 33 minutes. Remove the pan to a rack and let stand until completely cool. Using the overhanging foil as handles, lift the blondie to a cutting board. Carefully peel off the foil. Cut into bars.

HOW TO LINE BAKING PANS

A number of bar recipes call for lining the pan with aluminum foil, leaving enough overhang on two opposing ends to use as handles. Foil not only makes cleaning up easy, but also means the cooled slab can be lifted from the pan and transferred to a board for cutting in one fell swoop.

1 The easiest way to shape the foil is to turn the pan upside down, then smooth the foil around the contours of the pan until the right shape is achieved.

2 Turn the pan right side up and fit the foil inside.

Chocolate and Cocoa

Chocolate comes from almond-shaped beans that grow inside the pods of cacao trees in tropical areas near the equator. Cocoa beans (**1**), as they are known in the United States, develop their distinctive chocolate flavor, color, and aroma only after they have been fermented, dried, and roasted. To make chocolate, the roasted beans are chopped into small pieces called nibs. The nibs are rich in cocoa butter, a cream-colored, natural vegetable fat that melts during the grinding process producing a dark brown, fluid mass called chocolate liquor—the primary ingredient in all forms of chocolate (except white chocolate).

Chocolate liquor, also known as unsweetened, bitter, baking, or cooking chocolate, is pure chocolate with no added ingredients. It contains nearly equal parts cocoa butter and cocoa solids, the meat of the cocoa bean, which is why it imparts such a deep, rich chocolate flavor to anything you make with it. Unsweetened chocolate is always combined with sugar to make American-style cakes, brownies, frostings, and fudges.

Extra-bittersweet, bittersweet (**2**), semisweet, and sweet cooking chocolates are made of chocolate liquor, not more than 12 percent milk solids, cocoa butter, sugar, vanilla or vanillin, and lecithin. Bittersweet bars often have a deeper chocolate flavor than those labeled "semisweet," and they are apt to be less sweet (although the amount of sugar they contain is not regulated). These chocolates may be used interchangeably in most recipes, but their differences can alter the flavor, texture, and appearance of the finished product. For that reason, try to use the chocolate specified in the recipe.

Milk chocolate, America's favorite eating chocolate, is the sweetest of the sweet chocolates. It is lighter in color and less intensely chocolate flavored than dark chocolate because it contains less chocolate liquor and at least 3.39 percent butterfat and 12 percent milk solids. Milk chocolate is rarely used for baking because of its high sugar content and heat-sensitive milk solids.

Cocoa (**3**) is pulverized, partially defatted chocolate liquor that contains 10 to 24 percent cocoa butter and absolutely no sugar. Two types of cocoa are available in supermarkets: nonalkalized (natural) and alkalized (Dutch-process). Nonalkalized cocoa is light in color and somewhat acidic with a strong, assertive chocolate flavor. Alkalized, or Dutch-process, cocoa has been processed with alkali to neutralize its natural acidity by raising its pH level. It is darker, milder in taste, and less acidic than nonalkalized cocoa. When buying Dutch-process cocoa, look for labels that say Dutch-process or European-style. Don't confuse cocoa powder, which is unsweetened, with instant cocoa, which usually contains 80 percent sugar, is precooked, and has an emulsifier added to make it dissolve readily. In baking, use nonalkalized cocoa in recipes that call for baking soda and alkalized cocoa in those that use baking powder as the primary leavener. In recipes where no leavening is required, the choice is a matter of taste and we call simply for unsweetened cocoa.

Raspberry Brownies Cockaigne

Twenty-four 2¼ x 2-inch bars

Raspberries and chocolate are one of our favorite flavor combinations, and this voluptuous new recipe well deserves the Cockaigne name. If you like cakey brownies, mix the batter with an electric mixer. If you prefer fudgy brownies, mix everything by hand with a whisk.

Position a rack in the center of the oven. Preheat the oven to 350°F. Line a 13 x 9-inch baking pan with greased aluminum foil, allowing it to overhang the 2 narrow ends of the pan by about 2 inches.

Melt, stirring constantly, in a small, heavy saucepan over very low heat:

12 ounces unsweetened chocolate, coarsely chopped

¾ pound (3 sticks) unsalted butter

Remove from the heat and whisk until smooth. Let cool to room temperature. Beat with a wooden spoon until well combined:

6 large eggs

3 cups sugar

2 teaspoons vanilla

Fold in the cooled chocolate mixture. Sift over the top and stir in just until combined:

1½ cups all-purpose flour

Scrape the batter into the pan and spread to the edges. Drop by teaspoonfuls evenly over the top:

⅔ cup raspberry jam

Insert the tip of a knife ½ inch into the batter, then evenly distribute the jam by swirling the knife. Bake until the center of the top is almost firm when lightly pressed and a toothpick inserted in the center comes out clean but still moist at the bottom, 30 to 35 minutes. Remove the pan to a rack and let stand until completely cool. Using the overhanging foil as handles, lift the brownie to a cutting board. Cutting this brownie into bars can be messy, so refrigerate the cooled slab for about 1 hour before slicing. Carefully peel off the foil. Cut into bars.

STIRRING INGREDIENTS INTO A BATTER

Stirring is used to incorporate dry and/or wet ingredients gently but thoroughly into another mixture, without overmixing or beating, which may toughen the mixture by developing the gluten in the flour.

To stir by hand, use a wooden spoon or rubber spatula. Begin at the center of the bowl, mixing with a circular motion in an ever-widening pattern as the ingredients become blended. Scrape the sides of the bowl from time to time as necessary. Alternatively, to stir with an electric mixer, use low speed and mix just until the ingredients are smoothly blended. Do not overdo it. Scrape the sides of the bowl with a rubber spatula as necessary.

Cheesecake Brownies

Sixteen 2 x 2-inch bars

Set cream cheese out to soften before beginning to prepare these.

Position a rack in the center of the oven. Preheat the oven to 350°F. Line an 8 x 8-inch baking pan with greased aluminum foil, allowing it to overhang 2 opposing ends of the pan by about 2 inches.

Whisk together thoroughly:

1 cup all-purpose flour
¼ teaspoon salt
¼ teaspoon baking soda

Melt, stirring constantly, in a large, heavy saucepan over very low heat:

6 ounces bittersweet chocolate, or 5½ ounces semisweet and ½ ounce unsweetened chocolate, coarsely chopped
4 tablespoons (½ stick) unsalted butter

Let cool to barely warm. Add and beat with a wooden spoon until well blended:

⅔ cup sugar
2½ teaspoons vanilla

Beat in 1 at a time until well combined:

2 large eggs

Stir in:

2 tablespoons light corn syrup

Stir the flour mixture into the chocolate mixture until well blended and smooth. Scrape the batter into the pan and spread to the edges. Bake for 12 minutes.

Meanwhile, combine in a food processor until well blended:

12 ounces (1½ packages) cream cheese, softened and cut into chunks
½ cup sugar
2 tablespoons unsalted butter, melted
1 large egg
1 teaspoon vanilla
¼ teaspoon finely grated lemon zest

Spread the cream cheese topping evenly over the chocolate layer. Reduce the oven temperature to 325°F.

Return the pan to the oven. Bake until the cheesecake layer is just tinged with brown and beginning to crack on top and a toothpick inserted in the center comes out clean but still moist and fudgy at the bottom, 32 to 36 minutes. Remove the pan to a rack and let stand until completely cool. Refrigerate until well chilled before slicing. Using the overhanging foil as handles, lift the brownie to a cutting board. Carefully peel off the foil. Cut into bars (opposite).

Chewy Brownies (Reduced Fat)

Twelve 2¾ x 2-inch bars

These brownies contain just under 4 grams of fat apiece.

Position a rack in the center of the oven. Preheat the oven to 350°F. Line an 8 x 8-inch baking pan with greased or nonstick spray–coated aluminum foil, allowing it to overhang 2 opposing ends of the pan by about 2 inches.

Whisk together thoroughly:

¾ cup all-purpose flour
1½ tablespoons unsweetened nonalkalized cocoa, sifted
¼ teaspoon baking soda
¼ teaspoon salt

Melt, stirring constantly, in a large, heavy saucepan over very low heat:

4 ounces semisweet or bittersweet chocolate, coarsely chopped
2 teaspoons corn or canola oil

Remove from the heat and stir in until well combined:

½ cup packed light brown sugar
¼ cup sugar
2 tablespoons light corn syrup
1 tablespoon water
2 teaspoons vanilla

Add and stir until the sugar is dissolved:

2 large egg whites

Stir the flour mixture into the chocolate mixture until well blended and smooth.

Scrape the batter into the pan and spread to the edges. Bake until the center of the top is almost firm when lightly pressed and a toothpick inserted in the center comes out clean but still moist and fudgy at the bottom, 20 to 25 minutes. Remove the pan to a rack and let stand until completely cool. Using the overhanging foil as handles, lift the brownie to a cutting board. Carefully peel off the foil. Cut into bars.

Spiced Apple Bars ❄

Eighteen 3 x 2-inch bars

These bars (opposite left) go wonderfully with homemade eggnog.
Position a rack in the center of the oven. Preheat the oven to 350°F.
Line a 13 x 9-inch baking pan with greased aluminum foil, allowing it to overhang the 2 narrow ends of the pan by about 2 inches.
In a large saucepan over low heat, melt:

½ pound (2 sticks) unsalted butter
Remove from the heat and stir in:
1⅓ cups packed dark brown sugar

1 cup sugar
Add:
4 large eggs
½ teaspoon vanilla
Stir together with a wire whisk and then add:
2⅔ cups all-purpose flour
2½ teaspoons baking powder
1 teaspoon ground cinnamon
½ teaspoon ground ginger
Stir in:
2½ cups coarsely grated peeled apples (about 5 medium)

1½ cups golden raisins
Scrape the batter into the pan and spread to the edges. Bake until firm and a toothpick inserted in the center comes out slightly wet, 30 to 35 minutes. Remove the pan to a rack and let stand until completely cool. Using the overhanging foil as handles, lift the bar to a cutting board. Carefully peel off the foil. Cut into bars.

Lemon Curd Bars Cockaigne

Eighteen 3 x 2-inch bars

Our family loves lemon in any form but is especially partial to these bars. We like to sift powdered sugar over the tops (opposite right).
Position a rack in the center of the oven. Preheat the oven to 325°F.
Have ready a 13 x 9-inch baking pan. Sift together into a large bowl:

1½ cups all-purpose flour
¼ cup powdered sugar
Sprinkle over the top:
12 tablespoons (1½ sticks) cold unsalted butter, cut into small pieces

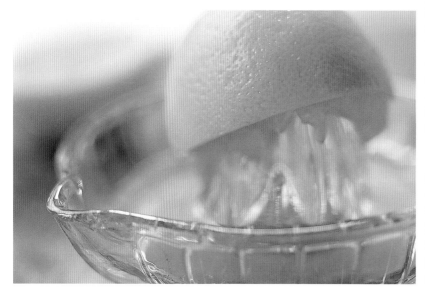

Using a pastry blender, 2 knives, or your fingertips, cut in the butter until the mixture is the size of small peas. Using your fingers, press the mixture into the bottom of the pan and ¾ inch up the sides to avoid leaking during baking. Bake until golden brown, 20 to 30 minutes. Set aside to cool slightly. Reduce the oven temperature to 300°F. Whisk together until well combined:

6 large eggs
3 cups sugar
Stir in:
Grated zest of 1 lemon
1 cup plus 2 tablespoons fresh lemon juice (about 5 lemons)
Sift over the top and stir in until well blended and smooth:
½ cup all-purpose flour
Pour the batter over the baked crust. Bake until set, about 35 minutes. Remove the pan to a rack to cool completely before cutting into bars.

Raspberry Streusel Bars

Twenty 2½ x 2¼-inch bars

Generously grease a 13 x 9-inch baking pan.

Sift together into a large bowl:

2 cups all-purpose flour

¼ cup sugar

¼ teaspoon salt

Sprinkle over the top:

12 tablespoons (1½ sticks) cold unsalted butter, cut into small pieces

Using a pastry blender, 2 knives, or your fingertips, cut in the butter until the mixture resembles fine crumbs. Stir together:

3 tablespoons milk

1 teaspoon almond extract

Sprinkle the milk mixture over the flour mixture. Lightly stir to blend. Knead until the milk is distributed and the particles begin to hold together. If necessary, add a teaspoon or two more milk, until the mixture holds together but is not wet. (Alternatively, in a food processor, process the dry ingredients and butter in on/off pulses until the mixture resembles coarse crumbs; be careful not to overprocess. A bit at a time, add the milk mixture, and process in on/off pulses until the particles begin to hold together; if necessary, add just enough additional milk so the mixture holds together but is not wet.)

Firmly press the dough into the pan to form a smooth, even layer. Refrigerate for 15 minutes. Meanwhile, position a rack in the center of the oven and another in the upper third. Preheat the oven to 375°F.

Bake the chilled dough in the center of the oven until barely firm in the center, 12 to 15 minutes. Spread evenly over the hot crust:

1 cup seedless raspberry preserves or jam

To prepare the streusel, whisk together thoroughly:

1¾ cups all-purpose flour

⅔ cup sugar

½ teaspoon ground cinnamon

¼ teaspoon salt

Sprinkle over the top:

8 tablespoons (1 stick) cold unsalted butter, cut into small pieces

Using a pastry blender, 2 knives, or your fingertips, cut in the butter until the mixture is well blended. (Alternatively, combine the flour, sugar, cinnamon, and salt in a food processor. Sprinkle the butter over the top. Process until the mixture is well blended. Turn out into a bowl.) Using a fork, stir into the flour mixture 1 at a time:

¾ cup sliced blanched or natural (unblanched) almonds

½ cup old-fashioned rolled oats

Beat together lightly and stir into the flour mixture until the streusel is moistened and forms small clumps:

1 large egg

2 tablespoons milk

(If necessary, add a teaspoon or two more milk, until the mixture is just moist enough to clump.) Sprinkle the streusel evenly over the raspberry preserves, breaking up any large clumps with a fork or your fingertips. Bake in the upper third of the oven until the streusel is nicely browned and the raspberry mixture is bubbly, 25 to 30 minutes. Remove the pan to a rack to cool completely. Cut into bars.

Dream Bars (Angel Bars)

Twelve 2¾ x 2⅓-inch bars

Many a copy of Joy has been sold on the strength of this recipe, or so we have been told.

Have all ingredients at room temperature, 68° to 70°F. Position a rack in the center of the oven. Preheat the oven to 350°F. Line an 11 x 7-inch or similar 2-quart rectangular baking pan with greased aluminum foil, allowing it to overhang the 2 narrow ends of the pan by about 2 inches. Beat on medium speed until very fluffy and well blended:

4 tablespoons (½ stick) unsalted butter, softened
2 tablespoons sugar
1 large egg yolk
¼ teaspoon vanilla

Stir in, then knead until well blended and smooth:

¾ cup all-purpose flour

Firmly press the dough into the pan to form a smooth, even layer. Bake for 10 minutes; set aside to cool slightly.

Toast, stirring occasionally, in a baking pan until the coconut is very lightly browned, 7 to 10 minutes:

1½ cups chopped pecans or walnuts
1 cup flaked or shredded sweetened coconut

Beat on medium speed or with a wooden spoon until well combined:

2 large eggs
1 cup packed light brown sugar
1½ tablespoons all-purpose flour
¼ teaspoon baking powder
⅛ teaspoon salt
1½ teaspoons vanilla

Stir the nut mixture into the egg mixture. Spread the mixture evenly over the baked layer. Bake until the top is firm and golden brown and a toothpick inserted in the center comes out slightly wet, 20 to 25 minutes. Remove the pan to a rack to cool slightly. While the bar is still warm, stir together:

2 tablespoons unsalted butter, softened
⅔ cup powdered sugar
2 teaspoons fresh lemon juice
½ teaspoon vanilla

If necessary, stir in enough water to yield a spreadable consistency. Spread the icing evenly over the top. Let stand until completely cool and the icing is set. Using the overhanging foil as handles, lift the bar to a cutting board. Carefully peel off the foil. Cut into bars.

Rocky Road Bars

Eighteen 3 x 2-inch bars

Three kinds of chocolate are used in this recipe. For instructions on how to melt chocolate, see page 51.

Position a rack in the center of the oven. Preheat the oven to 350°F. Line a 13 x 9-inch baking pan with greased aluminum foil, allowing it to overhang the 2 narrow ends of the pan by about 2 inches.

Melt, stirring often, in the top of a double boiler or in a microwave on medium power:

4 ounces unsweetened chocolate

Remove from the heat and, using a wire whisk, beat until smooth. Cool to room temperature.

Using an electric mixer, beat together until smooth:

8 tablespoons (1 stick) unsalted butter, softened
1½ cups sugar

Beat in:

4 large eggs
1 teaspoon vanilla

With a wooden spoon, fold in the cooled chocolate. Sift over, then stir to blend:

¾ cup all-purpose flour
2 tablespoons unsweetened cocoa
⅛ teaspoon salt

In a separate bowl, mix together:

1 cup coarsely chopped walnuts or pecans
1 cup mini marshmallows
1 cup semisweet chocolate chips

Stir all but 1 cup of the nut mixture into the batter until well combined. Scrape the batter into the pan and spread to the edges. Sprinkle the remaining nut mixture over the top. Bake until the top is firm when lightly tapped and a toothpick inserted in the center comes out slightly wet, about 25 minutes. Remove the pan to a rack and let stand until completely cool. Using the overhanging foil as handles, lift the bar to a cutting board. Carefully peel off the foil. Cut into bars.

Chocolate-Glazed Toffee Bars ❄

Twenty-four 2 x 1⅓-inch bars

A cookie made up of a chewy brown sugar-pecan toffee layer spread over shortbread and topped with chocolate.
Grease an 8 x 8-inch baking pan. Whisk together thoroughly:

⅔ cup all-purpose flour

1½ tablespoons sugar

⅛ teaspoon salt

Sprinkle over the top:

4 tablespoons (½ stick) cold unsalted butter, cut into small pieces

Using a pastry blender, 2 knives, or your fingertips, cut in the butter until the mixture resembles fine crumbs. Sprinkle over the top and stir in to blend:

2 teaspoons milk

Knead until the milk is distributed and the particles begin to hold together. If necessary, add a teaspoon or two more milk, until the mixture holds together but is not wet. (Alternatively, in a food processor, process the dry ingredients and butter in on/off pulses until the mixture resembles coarse crumbs; be careful not to overprocess. A bit at a time, add the milk, and process in on/off pulses until the particles begin to hold together; if necessary, add just enough additional milk so the mixture holds together but is not wet.) Firmly press the dough into the pan to form a smooth, even layer. Refrigerate for 15 minutes. Meanwhile, position a rack in the center of the oven. Preheat the oven to 350°F.

Bake the chilled dough for 10 minutes; set aside to cool slightly. Toast, stirring occasionally in a baking pan, until very lightly browned, 5 to 8 minutes:

1½ cups chopped pecans

Set aside to cool. Combine in a medium, heavy saucepan and, stirring frequently, bring to a boil over medium heat:

5 tablespoons unsalted butter, cut into pieces

½ cup packed light brown sugar

2 tablespoons clover or other mild honey

1 tablespoon milk

⅛ teaspoon salt

Boil the mixture, uncovered, for 3 minutes; remove from the heat. Stir in the toasted pecans along with:

1 teaspoon vanilla

Spread the mixture evenly over the baked layer. Bake until the crumb mixture is bubbly, golden brown, and just slightly darker at the edges, 17 to 20 minutes. Remove the pan to a rack to cool slightly. Sprinkle over the top:

¼ cup semisweet chocolate chips

Let stand for several minutes until the chocolate chips partially melt, then smooth across the surface with a table knife to partially spread the chocolate. (The surface should not be completely covered with chocolate.) Sprinkle over the top:

2 tablespoons finely chopped pecans

Let the chocolate cool until thickened but still slightly soft, then cut into bars; let cool completely before lifting the bars from the pan. Retrace the initial cuts to separate the bars, if necessary.

HOW TO MELT CHOCOLATE

Chocolate is heat-sensitive and burns easily, especially when melted alone. Do not heat dark chocolate over 120°F or milk and white chocolates over 110°F. White chocolate is the most delicate of all. Containers and stirring utensils must be clean and perfectly dry; stray drops of water or condensation must not be allowed to touch the chocolate. Small amounts of water may cause melted chocolate to lose its gloss and tighten or "seize" instead of melting smoothly.

1 Chop the chocolate into almond-sized pieces with a sharp, dry knife.

2 To melt chocolate using a water bath, place one-third of it in the top of a double boiler or in a bowl that fits snugly over the top of a saucepan. Fill the bottom pan with enough hot tap water (130°F) to touch the bottom of the top bowl, but not so much as to allow the bowl to float. Avoid splashing water into it. Begin stirring with a rubber spatula when the outside edges of the chocolate begin to liquefy. Gradually add the rest of the chocolate. Carefully lift the bowl of chocolate from the water bath when the chocolate is nearly melted, dry the bottom, and continue stirring the chocolate until it is smooth and shiny.

To melt chocolate using the microwave, select a dry, microwave-safe plastic bowl and fill it no more than half full with chopped chocolate. Microwave 1 to 8 ounces of dark chocolate, uncovered, on medium for 1½ to 3½ minutes, depending on the amount. Use low power for milk and white chocolates. Stir it after the first 1½ minutes, even if it appears firm. If necessary, continue microwaving in increasingly shorter increments at the appropriate power level until most of the chocolate is melted. Stir until the chocolate is smooth and shiny.

Candy Bar Bars ❄

Eighteen 3 x 2-inch bars

We like to use crunchy toffee bars, but feel free to substitute your favorite kind. If using creamy caramel candy bars, freeze them before chopping.

Position a rack in the center of the oven. Preheat the oven to 350°F. Line a 13 x 9-inch baking pan with greased aluminum foil, allowing it to overhang the 2 narrow ends of the pan by about 2 inches.

Using an electric mixer, beat together until smooth:

18 tablespoons (2¼ sticks) unsalted butter, softened

1½ cups sugar

Beat in:

2 large eggs

¾ teaspoon vanilla

Sift over, then stir to blend:

3 cups all-purpose flour

¾ teaspoon baking soda

¼ teaspoon salt

Add and stir to combine:

10 ounces candy bars, chopped into ½-inch pieces

Scrape the batter into the pan and spread to the edges. Bake until the top is firm when lightly tapped and a toothpick inserted in the center comes out slightly wet, 25 to 30 minutes. Remove the pan to a rack and let stand until completely cool. Using the overhanging foil as handles, lift the bar to a cutting board. Carefully peel off the foil. Cut into bars.

Congo Bars

Eighteen 3 x 2-inch bars

Position a rack in the center of the oven. Preheat the oven to 350°F. Line a 13 x 9-inch baking pan with greased aluminum foil, allowing it to overhang the 2 narrow ends of the pan by about 2 inches.

In a large saucepan over low heat, melt:

½ pound (2 sticks) unsalted butter

Remove from the heat and stir in:

2⅓ cups packed dark brown sugar

Stir in until well combined:

4 large eggs

1 teaspoon vanilla

Sift over, then stir in:

2⅔ cups all-purpose flour

2½ teaspoons baking powder

Stir in:

2 cups semisweet chocolate chips

1½ cups chopped walnuts

½ cup flaked or shredded sweetened coconut (optional)

Scrape the batter into the pan and spread to the edges. Bake until firm when lightly tapped and a toothpick inserted in the center comes out slightly wet, about 25 minutes. Remove the pan to a rack and let stand until completely cool. Using the overhanging foil as handles, lift the bar to a cutting board. Carefully peel off the foil. Cut into bars.

MOCHA JAVA CONGO BARS

Eighteen 3 x 2-inch bars

Prepare *Congo Bars, above,* adding 4 teaspoons instant espresso granules or powder with the flour and baking powder.

Peanut Butter Chocolate Bars

Eighteen 3 x 2-inch bars

These lush bar cookies are the "fastest" we know, since they are scarfed up as quickly as we can make them.

Position a rack in the center of the oven. Preheat the oven to 325°F. Have ready a 13 x 9-inch baking pan.

In a medium, heavy saucepan over low heat, melt:

10 tablespoons (1¼ sticks) unsalted butter

Add and stir until combined:

2 cups finely ground chocolate cookie crumbs

Using your fingers, press the mixture evenly into the bottom of the pan. Bake until dry, about 15 minutes. Set aside to cool slightly. Using an electric mixer, beat together until smooth:

1 pound cream cheese

⅔ cup sugar

Beat in:

2 large eggs

Stir in until the mixture is smooth:

¾ cup smooth peanut butter

With a rubber spatula, spread the mixture evenly over the baked crust.

Bake until set, 10 to 15 minutes. Remove the pan to a rack to cool to room temperature.

Bring just to a boil:

½ cup heavy cream

Remove from the heat and add:

3½ ounces bittersweet or semi-sweet chocolate, finely chopped

Using a wire whisk, beat until smooth. With a rubber spatula, spread the chocolate mixture evenly over the peanut butter mixture. Refrigerate until firm. Cut into bars.

Mother Kroll's Lebkuchen ❄

Twenty-four 2 x 2-inch bars

These German cookies date back to the Middle Ages, when honey was the everyday sweetener. This recipe was given to us by Carolyn Reidy, the president of our publishing company. Carolyn's mother, Mildred Kroll, comes from a long line of cookie bakers, and this is a family favorite at Christmas.

Position a rack in the center of the oven. Preheat the oven to 400°F. Line a 13 x 9-inch baking pan with greased aluminum foil, allowing it to overhang the 2 narrow ends of the pan by about 2 inches.

Bring to a boil in a large, heavy saucepan:

1 cup honey

Remove from the heat and let cool completely. Stir in:

¾ cup packed light or dark brown sugar
1 large egg, lightly beaten
1 tablespoon fresh lemon juice

1 teaspoon grated lemon zest

Combine and sift over the honey mixture:

2½ cups sifted all-purpose flour
½ teaspoon baking soda
1 teaspoon ground cinnamon
½ teaspoon ground allspice
½ teaspoon ground nutmeg
¼ teaspoon ground cloves

Stir together:

⅓ cup chopped blanched almonds
⅓ cup chopped citron

Add to the honey mixture and stir until well blended. Firmly press the dough into the pan to form a smooth, even layer. Bake until a toothpick inserted in the center comes out almost clean, 18 to 20 minutes.

Meanwhile, stir together until smooth:

1 cup powdered sugar
2 tablespoons fresh lemon juice

¼ teaspoon vanilla

If necessary, stir in enough water to yield a spreadable consistency. While the bar is still warm, spread the icing evenly over the top. Immediately mark into 24 squares and decorate by placing in the center of each square:

1 candied cherry

Arrange around each cherry in an X shape originating from each corner:

4 whole blanched almonds

Remove the pan to a rack and let stand until completely cool and the icing is set. Using the overhanging foil as handles, lift the bar to a cutting board. Carefully peel off the foil. Cut into bars. If possible, let the cookies age for at least 2 weeks to allow the spices to ripen. Lebkuchen will keep for months in an airtight container.

Scottish Shortbread

Twenty-four 2 x 1⅓-inch bars

Fragrant with butter, this cookie (opposite front) is easy to make. Some shortbread lovers substitute rice flour or cornstarch for a portion of the all-purpose flour. Unlike wheat flour, rice flour and cornstarch do not develop gluten, and therefore produce an especially crumbly and tender shortbread. If desired, substitute ⅓ cup rice flour or cornstarch for an equal amount of all-purpose flour.

Position a rack in the center of the oven. Preheat the oven to 300°F. Have ready an 8 x 8-inch baking pan or a rectangular shortbread mold. Beat on medium speed until very fluffy and well blended:

10 tablespoons (1¼ sticks) unsalted butter, softened
¼ cup powdered sugar
1½ tablespoons sugar
¼ teaspoon salt

Gradually sift over the top while stirring:

1½ cups all-purpose flour

Lightly knead until well blended and smooth. If the dough is too dry to hold together, sprinkle a few drops of water over it, adding only enough to hold the particles together and being careful not to overmoisten it. Firmly press the dough into the pan or mold to form a smooth, even layer. If baking in a pan, pierce the dough deeply with a fork all over in a decorative pattern. Bake until the shortbread is faintly tinged with pale gold and just slightly darker at the edges, 45 to 50 minutes. Remove the pan to a rack and let cool until barely warm. Cut almost through the dough to form bars. If desired, sprinkle with:

1 to 2 teaspoons sugar

Let stand until completely cool. Gently retrace the cuts and separate into bars.

Chocolate Shortbread

Fifteen 3 x 2½-inch bars

Our friend Mildred Kroll used to make this quick version of shortbread (opposite center) as a snack for her kids when they went off to college.

Position a rack in the center of the oven. Preheat the oven to 300°F. Have ready a 13 x 9-inch baking pan. Beat on medium speed until very fluffy and well blended:

½ pound (2 sticks) unsalted butter, softened
½ cup superfine sugar

Melt, stirring often, in the top of a double boiler or in a microwave on medium:

2 ounces semisweet or bittersweet chocolate

Remove from the heat and let cool slightly. Sift over the top of the butter mixture:

2 cups all-purpose flour

Add the melted chocolate, then stir until well blended. Press the dough into the pan to form a smooth, even layer. Bake until the top is firm when lightly pressed and a toothpick inserted in the center comes out clean, about 40 minutes. Remove the pan to a rack and let cool until barely warm. Cut into bars and transfer to a rack to cool.

PETTICOAT TAILS

12 wedges

This traditional British shortbread may get its name from the fact that it's baked in a round pan and cut into fan-shaped wedges—said to resemble the bell-hoop petticoats worn by royal ladies in the 18th century. On the other hand, the name might also derive from the French term petits gâteaux, *or little cakes.*

Prepare dough as for *Scottish Shortbread, left.*

Firmly press the dough in an even layer into an 8- to 8½-inch round cake pan or shortbread mold or fluted tart pan. If baking in a cake or tart pan, press the dough edge all the way around with the tines of a fork in a decorative pattern. Using a table knife, carefully cut the dough round into quarters. Then cut each quarter into thirds to yield 12 equal wedges. Decorate the surface by deeply piercing with a fork at even intervals. Bake as directed for *Scottish Shortbread, left.* Cool until barely warm. Gently retrace the cuts, then let stand in the pan until completely cool. Separate into wedges.

ABOUT **ROLLED** COOKIES

*S*ugar cookies and gingerbread people are the best-known rolled cookies, but many ethnic and regional specialties, such as Moravian Molasses Thins *and* Sablés, 68, *are shaped by this method, too.*

To turn out first-rate rolled cookies, the dough needs to be firm and manageable enough to roll and cut out easily. Avoid overflouring or overworking the dough, though; inexperienced bakers often ruin rolled cookies by using too much flour in the rolling process. See Rules for Rolling Dough, 65.

Rolled cookies are usually cut into shapes with cookie cutters. These can be fun to collect, and an interesting assortment of cutters makes it possible to turn out eye-catching cookies with no extra effort. The rim of a glass or cup can be used if necessary, but it won't provide the variety of shapes or give the sharp, clean edges good tin cutters do. A compromise is to cut the rolled-out dough into diamonds, squares, triangles, or other geometric shapes with a sharp knife.

Iced Sugar Cookies, 60

59

Iced Sugar Cookies ❄

About 3 dozen 2-inch cookies

These sugar cookies take well to decorative icing.

Whisk together thoroughly:

3¼ cups all-purpose flour

1½ teaspoons baking powder

½ teaspoon salt

Beat on medium speed until very fluffy and well blended:

20 tablespoons (2½ sticks) unsalted butter, softened

1 cup sugar

Add and beat until well combined:

1 large egg

1 tablespoon milk

2½ teaspoons vanilla

¼ teaspoon finely grated lemon zest (optional)

Gradually stir the flour mixture into the butter mixture until well blended and smooth. Divide the dough in half. Place each half between 2 large sheets of wax or parchment paper. Roll out to a scant ¼ inch thick, checking the underside of the dough and smoothing any creases. Keeping the paper in place, layer the rolled dough on a baking sheet and refrigerate until cold and slightly firm, about 30 minutes.

Position a rack in the center of the oven. Preheat the oven to 375°F. Grease cookie sheets.

Working with 1 portion at a time (leave the other refrigerated), gently peel away and replace 1 sheet of the paper. (This will make it easier to lift the cookies from the paper later.) Peel away and discard the second sheet. Cut out the cookies using 2-inch cutters. With a spatula, transfer them to the cookie sheets, spacing about 1½ inches apart. Roll the dough scraps and continue cutting out cookies until all the dough is used; briefly refrigerate the dough if it becomes too soft to handle.

If not planning to ice the cookies, decorate with:

Colored sugar or nonpareils

Bake, 1 sheet at a time, just until the cookies are lightly colored on top and slightly darker at the edges, 6 to 9 minutes; rotate the sheet halfway through baking for even browning. Remove the sheet to a rack and let stand until the cookies firm slightly. Transfer the cookies to racks to cool. Using a table knife, ice the top of each cookie with:

Quick Cookie Icing, 12

MAKING A TEMPLATE

Trace each figure on a separate piece of paper. You can also create your own shapes—for instance, a tree, bell, or rocking horse. If desired, enlarge or reduce the image on a photocopier. Then cut out the shape, paste it to a sturdy piece of cardboard, and cut out the template.

To use the template, oil or grease one side lightly, then lay it gently, oiled or greased side down, on a portion of the rolled-out dough. Working carefully, cut around the template with a small, sharp paring knife, then remove the template and lift out the shaped dough.

Fourteen in One (Master Recipe) ❄

About 7 dozen 2½-inch cookies

Simplicity itself. We love this recipe, especially at holiday time, because from just one easy cookie dough, you can make fourteen kinds of cookies. Putting the sugar through a food processor gives these cookies a wonderful lightness and fineness of texture.

Have all ingredients at room temperature, 68° to 70°F. In a large bowl, beat on medium speed until very fluffy and well blended:

½ pound (2 sticks) unsalted butter, at room temperature

1 cup sugar, processed in a food processor for 30 seconds, or superfine sugar

½ teaspoon salt

Add and beat until well blended:

1 large egg yolk

Add and beat until well combined:

1 large egg

2 teaspoons vanilla

Reduce the speed to low and beat in just until combined:

2½ cups all-purpose flour

Divide the dough in half and wrap in plastic. Refrigerate until firm, at least 1 hour. (The dough can be refrigerated for up to 2 days or it can be double-wrapped and frozen for up to 1 month.)

To bake, position a rack in the upper third and another in the lower third of the oven. Preheat the oven to 375°F.

Remove 1 portion of the dough from the refrigerator and cut it in half. Return the unused portion to the refrigerator.

EITHER: Scoop the cookie dough into 1-tablespoon balls with a small ice cream scoop and roll each ball between your palms until smooth. Place the dough balls on parchment-lined cookie sheets, spacing about 2 inches apart. Using the bottom of a smooth, flour-coated glass, flatten each dough ball to about ⅛ inch thick.

OR: Lightly flour the work surface.

Roll the dough to ⅛ inch thick, using a spatula to loosen the dough. Sprinkle the surface lightly with flour as needed to keep the dough from sticking. Cut the dough into desired shapes. Place the dough shapes on parchment-lined cookie sheets, spacing about ½ inch apart. Get as many dough shapes as you can out of each sheet, because the dough should be rolled only 2 times. Discard any leftover dough after the second rolling, or form the leftover dough into balls and flatten them to about ⅛ inch thick.

Bake, 2 sheets at a time, until the cookies are evenly golden brown, 6 to 8 minutes; rotate the sheets halfway through baking for even browning. Using a thin-bladed spatula, immediately transfer the cookies to racks to cool to room temperature. Decorate the cooled cookies, if desired, and transfer to an airtight container.

GINGER COOKIES

Add 1 teaspoon ground ginger to the flour and stir 6 tablespoons finely minced candied ginger into the finished dough.

BUTTERSCOTCH COOKIES

Substitute 1 cup packed light brown sugar for the sugar.

COCONUT COOKIES

Toast coconut in a 325°F oven.
After toasting 1 cup flaked sweetened dried coconut, stir it into the finished dough.

LEMON BUTTER COOKIES

When grating citrus zest, remove just the top colored layer.
Add 2 teaspoons finely grated lemon zest to the butter mixture.

LEMON POPPY SEED COOKIES

Add 2 teaspoons finely grated lemon zest to the butter mixture and stir 2 tablespoons poppy seeds into the finished dough.

CORNMEAL CITRUS COOKIES

Add 1 teaspoon finely grated lemon or orange zest to the butter mixture and substitute 1 cup fine cornmeal for 1 cup of the flour.

CHOCOLATE-CINNAMON COOKIES

Add 1 ounce melted and cooled unsweetened chocolate to the butter mixture. Substitute ¼ cup unsweetened cocoa for ¼ cup of the flour, and add ¼ teaspoon ground cinnamon to the flour mixture.

MARBLE COOKIES

Stir 2 ounces melted and cooled semisweet or bittersweet chocolate into one-quarter of the dough. Divide the chocolate dough into 6 portions. Press into the remaining plain dough. Knead the doughs together to create a marbled effect.

ORANGE BUTTER COOKIES

Add 1 teaspoon finely grated orange zest to the butter mixture.

ORANGE-NUT COOKIES

Add 1 teaspoon finely grated orange zest and 1 cup finely ground walnuts, pecans, or skinned hazelnuts to the butter mixture.

SPICE COOKIES

Substitute 1 cup packed light brown sugar for the sugar, and add ¾ teaspoon ground cinnamon, ½ teaspoon ground ginger, ¼ teaspoon ground nutmeg, ¼ teaspoon ground allspice, and ⅛ teaspoon ground cloves to the flour.

PEANUT BUTTER COOKIES

Because of the extra fat from the peanut butter in this recipe, these cookies have a sandier, melt-in-your-mouth texture.
Cream ⅔ cup peanut butter with the butter mixture.

RAISIN-SPICE COOKIES

Prepare *Spice Cookies, above,* and stir ½ cup finely minced raisins or ½ cup dried currants into the finished dough.

Rich Rolled Sugar Cookies ❋

2½ to 3½ dozen 2½- to 3½-inch cookies

Christmas wouldn't be Christmas without an assortment of these. This is the dough just waiting for that collection of cookie cutters you have squirreled away. Have fun decorating the different shapes with colored sprinkles or sugar. For a more elaborate finish, pipe with Royal Icing, 12.

Beat on medium speed until very fluffy and well blended:

½ pound (2 sticks) unsalted butter, softened

⅔ cup sugar

Add and beat until well combined:

1 large egg

¼ teaspoon baking powder

⅛ teaspoon salt

1½ teaspoons vanilla

Stir in until well blended and smooth:

2⅓ cups all-purpose flour

Divide the dough in half. Place each half between 2 large sheets of wax or parchment paper. Roll out to a scant ¼ inch thick, checking the underside of the dough and smoothing any creases. Keeping the paper in place, layer the rolled dough on a baking sheet and refrigerate until cold and slightly firm but not hard, 20 to 30 minutes.

Position a rack in the upper third of the oven. Preheat the oven to 350°F. Grease cookie sheets.

Working with 1 portion of dough at a time (leave the other refrigerated), gently peel away and replace 1 sheet of the paper. (This will make it easier to lift the cookies from the paper later.) Peel away and discard the second sheet. Cut out the cookies using 2- or 3-inch cutters. With a spatula,

transfer them to the cookie sheets, spacing about 1 inch apart. Roll the dough scraps and continue cutting out cookies until all the dough is used; briefly refrigerate the dough if it becomes too soft to handle.

If desired, very lightly sprinkle the cookies with:

Colored sprinkles or colored sugar

Bake, 1 sheet at a time, just until the cookies are lightly colored on top and slightly darker at the edges, 6 to 9 minutes; rotate the sheet halfway through baking for even browning. Remove the sheet to a rack and let stand until the cookies firm slightly. Transfer the cookies to racks to cool. If desired, decorate with:

Royal Icing, 12

RULES FOR ROLLING DOUGH

● The secret to rolling dough is to lean into the pin rather than down on it. The goal is to enlarge the dough, not press and crush it. Use firm, decisive, sweeping strokes and try to get the job done as quickly as possible.

● Resist the temptation to add extra flour to make a cookie dough more manageable during shaping or rolling, as you might if you were making bread.

● To prevent most cookie doughs from sticking to your work surface and rolling pin, roll portions between sheets of wax or parchment paper, occasionally checking the underside of the paper and smoothing any creases, shown opposite. Then, keeping the paper attached, layer the dough on trays and chill until slightly firm. Molasses doughs are too sticky to be rolled between paper, but letting them rest at room temperature for several hours before rolling out tames them enough to allow you to get by with minimal added flour.

● With short, rich doughs that seem too soft to handle, on the other hand, just the right amount of chilling will bring them under control. Refrigerate them until they are firm enough to hold their shape, but remove them before they become too cold and stiff. For doughs that warm up and soften very rapidly, start with only a portion of the dough, keeping the rest refrigerated until needed.

● When cutting or otherwise shaping cookies, try to keep them all about the same size and thickness, so that they bake evenly. And remember that if you choose to make cookies larger or smaller than the recipe specifies, the amount of spreading, the baking time, and the recipe yield will vary. The more you make cookies, the more adept you will become at dropping exact amounts of cookie dough and rolling dough to an even thickness each time, so that eventually your yields will be closer to those listed in the recipes.

ROLLING PINS

There are two kinds of rolling pins—the American pin with handles, and the European pole. If you have never rolled out crust before, choose an American pin of a size and weight you find comfortable. European rolling pins are made either thick and uniformly cylindrical or slender and tapered at the ends. Once you get the hang of rolling out dough, you will want a tapered pin for the way it allows you to maneuver the dough to any effect, but keep in mind that many beginners find tapered pins awkward to work with. Wood is the perfect material for all rolling pins. Hollow metal pins filled with ice water sweat; glass pins are beautiful to behold but are also fragile.

Gingerbread People (Reduced Fat) ❄

About 2 dozen 5-inch-tall cookies

No one would ever guess that one of these cookies contains only 3 grams of fat. If you like, make Quick Lemon Icing, 12, *or* Royal Icing, 12, *to decorate the cookies.*

Whisk together thoroughly:

3 cups all-purpose flour
1½ teaspoons baking powder
¾ teaspoon baking soda
¼ teaspoon salt
1 tablespoon ground ginger
1¾ teaspoons ground cinnamon
¼ teaspoon ground cloves

Using an electric mixer, beat on medium speed until well blended:

6 tablespoons (¾ stick) unsalted
**   butter, softened**
¾ cup packed dark brown sugar
1 large egg

Add and beat until well combined:

½ cup molasses
2 teaspoons vanilla
1 teaspoon finely grated
**   lemon zest**

Gradually stir in the dry ingredients until well blended and smooth. Divide the dough in half. Wrap each half in plastic and let stand at room temperature for at least 2 hours or up to 8 hours. (The dough can also be stored for up to 4 days, but in this case it should be refrigerated. Return to room temperature before using.)

To bake, position a rack in the upper third of the oven. Preheat the oven to 375°F. Grease cookie sheets. Place 1 portion of the dough on a lightly floured work surface. Very lightly sprinkle flour over the surface of the dough and dust the rolling pin. Roll out to a scant ¼ inch thick. Lift the dough frequently and add a bit more flour to the work surface and rolling pin as necessary to prevent sticking. Cut out the cookies using a 5-inch-tall gingerbread boy or girl cutter. With a spatula, transfer them to the cookie sheets, spacing about 1½ inches apart. Roll the dough scraps and continue cutting out cookies until all the dough is used.

If desired, garnish with:

Raisins and/or red hots, for eyes
**   and buttons**

Bake, 1 sheet at a time, until the edges of the cookies are just barely dark, 7 to 10 minutes; rotate the sheet halfway through baking for even browning. Remove the sheet to a rack and let stand until the cookies firm slightly. Transfer the cookies to racks to cool.

MAKING CHRISTMAS COOKIES INTO ORNAMENTS

To prepare a cookie ornament for hanging, use a toothpick to poke a hole through the uncooked shaped dough. When the cookie is baked, remove the toothpick, wiggling it a bit if necessary to widen the hole. Loop ribbon, colored yarn or string through the hole and tie in a pretty bow. The "snow"-covered gingerbread house, 114, also makes a charming decoration for the table or mantelpiece.

Sablés

About 4 dozen 2¼-inch cookies

Place in a large bowl:

½ pound (2 sticks) cold unsalted butter, cut into small pieces

2¾ cups all-purpose flour

Using a pastry blender, 2 knives, or your fingertips, cut in the butter until the mixture resembles fine crumbs. Beat together with a fork until well blended:

3 large egg yolks

¾ cup sugar

3 tablespoons powdered sugar

⅛ teaspoon salt

1½ teaspoons vanilla

2 or 3 drops almond extract (optional)

Stir the egg yolk mixture into the flour mixture, then knead to form a smooth dough. Divide the dough in half. Place each half between 2 large sheets of wax or parchment paper. Roll out to ¼ inch thick, checking the underside of the dough and smoothing any creases. Keeping the paper in place, layer the rolled dough on a baking sheet and freeze until cold and slightly firm, about 15 minutes. Position a rack in the upper third of the oven. Preheat the oven to 350°F. Grease cookie sheets. Working with 1 portion of dough at a time (leave the other in the freezer), gently peel away and replace 1 sheet of the paper. (This will make it easier to lift the cookies from the paper later.) Peel away and discard the second sheet.

Cut out the cookies using a fluted or plain round 2-inch or slightly larger cutter (or the rim of a glass). With a spatula, transfer them to the cookie sheets, spacing about 1 inch apart. Roll the dough scraps and continue cutting out cookies until all the dough is used; briefly refrigerate the dough if it becomes too soft to handle. Bake, 1 sheet at a time, just until the cookies are lightly colored on top and slightly darker at the edges, 12 to 16 minutes; rotate the sheet halfway through baking for even browning. Remove the sheet to a rack and let stand until the cookies firm slightly. Transfer the cookies (opposite back) to racks to cool.

Moravian Molasses Thins ❄

5½ to 7 dozen 2½-inch cookies

These gingery, paper-thin cookies are traditional in American communities settled by Moravian religious immigrants from central Europe. This recipe—an adaptation of one from Old Salem, North Carolina—has been modified to provide the option of substituting vegetable shortening, easier to find than good-quality lard. If you are adept at rolling the dough very thin, you may get 7 dozen cookies.

Whisk together thoroughly:

1 cup all-purpose flour

1½ teaspoons ground cinnamon

1 teaspoon ground ginger

½ teaspoon ground cloves

¼ teaspoon ground cardamom

½ teaspoon baking soda

Beat on medium speed until well blended:

⅓ cup molasses

¼ cup solid vegetable shortening or good-quality lard

½ cup packed dark brown sugar

1 teaspoon vanilla

Gradually stir the flour mixture into the molasses mixture, then knead until very smooth, 3 to 4 minutes. Divide the dough in half. Wrap each half in plastic and set aside in a cool spot (but not the refrigerator) for at least 6 hours and preferably 12 hours. (The dough can also be stored for up to 4 days, but in this case it should be refrigerated. Return to room temperature before using.) To bake, position a rack in the center of the oven. Preheat the oven to 300°F. Grease cookie sheets. Roll out half of the dough as thin as possible on a very lightly floured work surface. (The thinner the dough, the more cookies it will yield.) Lift the dough frequently and add a bit more flour to the work surface and rolling pin as necessary to prevent sticking. Cut out the cookies using a 2¼-inch fluted or plain round cutter. With a spatula, transfer them to the cookie sheets, spacing about 1 inch apart. Roll the dough scraps and continue cutting out cookies until all the dough is used.

Bake, 1 sheet at a time, until the edges of the cookies are just barely dark, 6 to 8 minutes; rotate the sheet halfway through baking for even browning. Don't overbake, as the cookies will be bitter. Remove the sheet to a rack and let stand until the cookies firm slightly. Transfer the cookies (opposite front) to racks to cool.

Cinnamon Stars ❄

About 2½ dozen 2½-inch star-shaped cookies

Most rolled doughs are flour-based, but these are made with meringue, resulting in chewy-crisp cookies with an intriguing spice and almond flavor. Cinnamon Stars are a Joy Christmas-time classic, often packed in gift tins, but always at the last minute, as they do not keep well.

Have all ingredients at room temperature, 68° to 70°F.

Position a rack in the center of the oven. Preheat the oven to 275°F. Grease and flour cookie sheets or cover with wax or parchment paper. Beat on medium speed until frothy:

3 large egg whites
⅛ teaspoon salt

Gradually add and beat until the egg whites are shiny and stiff:

2 cups powdered sugar, sifted

Remove a generous ½ cup of the meringue mixture, cover, and set aside to use as glaze.

Finely grind:

2½ cups slivered blanched almonds

Fold into the remaining meringue mixture until well blended along with:

1 tablespoon ground cinnamon
¾ teaspoon finely grated lemon zest

Heavily sprinkle over the top of the dough and gradually knead in:

½ to ⅔ cup powdered sugar (just enough to make the dough manageable)

Set the dough aside to rest for a few minutes.

Divide the dough in half. Place each half between 2 large sheets of wax or parchment paper. Roll out a scant ¼ inch thick, checking the underside of the dough and smoothing any creases. Working with 1 portion at a time, gently peel away and replace 1 sheet of the paper. (This will make it easier to lift the cookies from the paper later.) Peel away and discard the second sheet. Cut out the cookies using a 2½-inch star-shaped

cutter, dipping the cutter in powdered sugar occasionally to prevent sticking. With a spatula, transfer them to the cookie sheets, spacing about 2 inches apart. Roll the dough scraps and continue cutting out cookies until all the dough is used. Gradually stir into the reserved meringue mixture:

1 to 2½ teaspoons freshly squeezed lemon juice

Add enough juice to give the glaze a spreadable consistency. Ice the top of each star. Add a few drops of water to the glaze if it begins to dry out.

Bake, 1 sheet at a time, just until lightly colored and crispy on the outside, 27 to 32 minutes; rotate the pan halfway through baking. Remove the sheet to a rack and let stand until the cookies firm slightly. Transfer the cookies to racks to cool. Allow to mellow a few hours before serving.

Biscochitos (Southwest-Style Anise Sugar Cookies) ❄

About 3 dozen 2½-inch cookies

A great favorite in New Mexico.
Position a rack in the upper third of the oven. Preheat the oven to 375°F. Grease cookie sheets.
Thoroughly stir together and set aside:

2¼ cups all-purpose flour
2 teaspoons ground anise seeds, or 1½ teaspoons anise extract (add extract with the citrus zests)
½ teaspoon baking powder
¼ teaspoon salt

Using an electric mixer, beat until very fluffy and smooth:

½ cup lard or vegetable shortening
⅓ cup unsalted butter, softened
¾ cup sugar

Add and beat until smooth:

1 large egg

1 large egg yolk
¾ teaspoon grated lemon zest
½ teaspoon grated orange zest

Gradually beat the flour mixture into the butter mixture until well blended. Divide the dough in half. Place each half between 2 large sheets of wax or parchment paper. Roll out ⅛ inch thick, checking the underside of the dough and smoothing any creases. Keeping the paper in place, layer the rolled dough on a cookie sheet and refrigerate until chilled and slightly firm, 25 to 30 minutes.
Working with 1 portion of dough at a time (leave the other in the refrigerator), gently peel away and replace 1 sheet of the paper. (This will make

it easier to transfer the cookies later.) Peel away and discard the second sheet. Cut out the cookies using a 2½-inch cutter.
With a spatula, transfer the cookies to the cookie sheets, spacing about 1¼ inches apart. Roll the dough scraps and continue cutting out cookies until all the dough is used; briefly refrigerate the dough if it becomes too soft to handle. Lightly sprinkle the cookies with:

1 teaspoon ground cinnamon mixed with 2½ tablespoons sugar

Bake, 1 sheet at a time, until just tinged with brown at the edges, 7 to 9 minutes. Remove the sheet to a rack and let stand until slightly firm.

ABOUT
HAND-
SHAPED
COOKIES

*H*and-shaping is the art of forming dough into different shapes. It is the method that gives these cookies their certain character and personality.

It is important to note that the dough should be handled as little as possible. Warm hands can affect the texture of the cookies, especially those with a high butter content. Throughout this section we have illustrated some of the most common hand-shaping techniques. Many cookies begin as balls of dough that are rolled and then curved into crescents; flattened into rounds with the bottom of a glass, either oiled or dipped into sugar to prevent sticking; or pressed down with the tines of a fork, leaving an attractive crisscross pattern in the cookie surface. In the case of biscotti, dough is formed into logs or thin loaves, baked until almost firm, then cut crosswise on the diagonal into individual slices and baked again.

Clockwise from top left: Mandelbrezeln, 86; Glazed Lemon Dainties, 93; Classic Peanut Butter Cookies, 74

Classic Peanut Butter Cookies

About 3 dozen 2½-inch cookies

Position a rack in the upper third of the oven. Preheat the oven to 350°F. Grease cookie sheets.

Whisk together thoroughly:

2½ cups all-purpose flour
1¼ teaspoons baking powder
½ teaspoon baking soda
¼ teaspoon salt

Beat on medium speed until very fluffy and well blended:

¼ cup corn or canola oil
⅔ cup smooth peanut butter
12 tablespoons (1½ sticks)
**   unsalted butter, softened**
⅓ cup powdered sugar (sifted after
**   measuring if lumpy)**
1 cup packed light brown sugar

Add and beat until well combined:

1 large egg
1 large egg yolk
2½ teaspoons vanilla

Stir the flour mixture into the peanut butter mixture until well blended and smooth. Let the dough stand for about 5 minutes to firm slightly. Pull off pieces of the dough and roll between your palms into generous 1-inch balls; the dough will be fairly soft. Space about 2 inches apart on the sheets. Using the tines of a fork, form a crosshatch pattern and press each ball into a 1½-inch round, or use the bottom of a small glass to flatten each ball. Bake, 1 sheet at a time, until the cookies are just tinged with brown at the edges, 9 to 12 minutes; rotate the sheet halfway through baking for even browning. Remove the sheet to a rack and let stand until the cookies firm slightly. Transfer the cookies to racks to cool.

FLATTENING BALLS OF COOKIE DOUGH

While a good number of cookie doughs are soft enough to flatten once they hit the heat of the oven, some are firm enough to need some extra help. To ensure that the finished cookies made from firm doughs are evenly shaped, start by rolling the dough between the palms of your hands into neat balls. Set the balls on a cookie sheet and flatten them with the tines of a fork or with a small glass tumbler or measuring cup oiled or sugared lightly on the bottom, or dusted with flour or powdered sugar, or with cocoa for dark or chocolate doughs.

Snickerdoodles

About 3 dozen 3½-inch cookies

A New England favorite, these large, crinkly-topped sugar cookies are probably German in origin. Their name may be a corruption of the German word Schneckennudeln—which translates roughly as "crinkly noodles."

Position a rack in the upper third of the oven. Preheat the oven to 350°F. Grease cookie sheets.

Sift together:

2 cups all-purpose flour
2 teaspoons cream of tartar
1 teaspoon baking soda
¼ teaspoon salt

Beat on medium speed until very fluffy and well blended:

½ pound (2 sticks) unsalted butter, softened
1½ cups sugar

Add and beat until well combined:

2 large eggs

Stir the flour mixture into the butter mixture until well blended and smooth. Pull off pieces of the dough and roll between your palms to form generous 1¼-inch balls. Roll in a mixture of:

¼ cup sugar
4 teaspoons ground cinnamon

Space about 2¾ inches apart on the sheets. Bake, 1 sheet at a time, until the cookies are light golden brown at the edges, 8 to 11 minutes; rotate the sheet halfway through baking for even browning. Remove the sheet to a rack and let stand until the cookies firm slightly. Transfer the cookies to racks to cool. Let the cookie sheets cool between batches or the cookies may spread too much.

Orange Ginger Wafers (Reduced Fat)

About 4½ dozen 2½-inch wafers

These crispy wafers (opposite back) have less than 1.5 grams of fat each.

Position a rack in the upper third of the oven. Preheat the oven to 375°F. Coat cookie sheets with nonstick spray.

Whisk together thoroughly:

2 cups all-purpose flour
2 teaspoons baking powder
¼ teaspoon baking soda
½ teaspoon ground ginger
⅛ teaspoon ground cloves
¼ teaspoon salt

Beat on medium speed until well blended:

1 cup sugar
3 tablespoons corn or canola oil
2½ tablespoons unsalted butter, softened
2½ teaspoons finely grated orange zest
1 teaspoon finely grated lemon zest

Add and beat until well combined:

1 large egg
¼ cup light or dark molasses
2½ teaspoons vanilla

Gradually beat the flour mixture into the molasses mixture until well blended and smooth. Pull off pieces of the dough and roll between your palms into generous ¾-inch balls. Space about 2¼ inches apart on the sheets. Lightly oil the bottom of a large, flat-bottomed glass. Very lightly dip the glass into:

2 tablespoons sugar

Flatten the balls until ¼ inch thick, dipping the glass into the sugar before flattening each cookie. Wipe the buildup from the glass and oil as necessary. Bake, 1 sheet at a time, until the cookies are faintly tinged with brown and slightly darker at the edges, 8 to 11 minutes; rotate the sheet halfway through baking for even browning. Remove the sheet to a rack and let stand until the cookies firm slightly. Transfer the cookies to racks to cool. Let the cookie sheets cool between batches, or the cookies may spread too much.

Ginger Snaps

About 6 dozen 2¼-inch cookies

For very crunchy cookies, overbake slightly; for more tender ones, under-bake by a minute or two.

Position a rack in the upper third of the oven. Preheat the oven to 350°F. Grease cookie sheets.

Whisk together thoroughly:

3¾ cups all-purpose flour
1½ teaspoons baking powder
½ teaspoon baking soda
4 teaspoons ground ginger
1 teaspoon ground cinnamon
¼ teaspoon ground cloves
¼ teaspoon salt

Beat on medium speed until very fluffy and well blended:

12 tablespoons (1½ sticks) unsalted butter, softened
1⅔ cups sugar

Add and beat until well combined:

2 large eggs
½ cup dark molasses
2 teaspoons fresh lemon juice
¼ teaspoon finely grated lemon or orange zest

Stir the flour mixture into the molasses mixture until well blended and smooth. Pull off pieces of the dough and roll between your palms into generous 1-inch balls. Space about 1½ inches apart on the sheets. Pat down the balls to flatten the tops just slightly.

Bake, 1 sheet at a time, until the cookies are tinged with brown and just firm when lightly pressed in the center of the top, 10 to 13 minutes; rotate the sheet halfway through baking for even browning. (The cookies flatten and develop cracks during baking.) Remove the sheet to a rack and let stand until the cookies firm slightly. Transfer the cookies (opposite front) to racks to cool.

Chocolate Chip Cookies Cockaigne

About 3 dozen 2½-inch cookies

Finely ground rolled oats give the classic American cookie (opposite) a chewy crunch.

Position a rack in the upper third of the oven. Preheat the oven to 375°F. Grease cookie sheets.

Whisk together thoroughly:

1⅔ cups all-purpose flour
1¼ teaspoons baking soda
¾ teaspoon baking powder
¼ teaspoon salt

Beat on medium speed until lightened in color and creamy:

½ pound (2 sticks) unsalted butter, softened

Add and beat until well blended:

¾ cup sugar
⅔ cup packed light brown sugar
1 large egg
1½ tablespoons milk
2½ teaspoons vanilla

Stir the flour mixture into the butter mixture until well blended and smooth. Finely grind in a food processor or blender:

1⅓ cups old-fashioned rolled oats

Stir into the dough along with:

1 cup semisweet chocolate chips
One 3-ounce milk chocolate bar, coarsely grated or finely chopped
¾ cup chopped walnuts or pecans (optional)

With lightly greased hands, shape the dough into generous 1½-inch balls. Space about 2 inches apart on the sheets. Pat down the tops of the balls just slightly.

Bake, 1 sheet at a time, just until the cookies are tinged with brown, 8 to 12 minutes; rotate the sheet halfway through baking for even browning. Be careful not to over-bake. (The cookies should be soft in the center.) Remove the sheet to a rack and let stand until the cookies firm slightly. Transfer the cookies to racks to cool.

Peanut Butter Chubbies

About 24 1¼-inch cookies

These intensely flavored peanut butter shortbread cookies are tender almost to the point of being crumbly. Peanut Butter Chubbies have a distinctive and appealing taste that comes from the addition of peanut butter cups to the dough. Because the cookies must be completely cooled on the baking sheet before they are removed, using your largest cookie sheet and baking all the dough in one batch is recommended. However, baking in two batches, using two cookie sheets, works as well.

Position a rack in the center of the oven. Preheat the oven to 350°F. Grease a very large cookie sheet.

Whisk together thoroughly:

1 cup all-purpose flour
¼ teaspoon salt

Add and beat on low speed until the mixture just begins to hold together:

5½ tablespoons (⅔ stick) cold unsalted butter, cut into small pieces
3 tablespoons smooth or chunky peanut butter
½ teaspoon vanilla

Add and beat until well blended:

11 ounces peanut butter cups, chopped (about 14 peanut butter cups)
⅔ cup finely chopped unsalted peanuts

Shape into 1-inch balls. Space about 1¼ inches apart on the baking sheet. Bake until faintly tinged with brown, 15 to 18 minutes; rotate the sheet halfway through baking for even browning. Remove the sheet to a rack and let stand until the cookies are completely cool and firm; do not attempt to move the cookies beforehand, as they will be too crumbly.

Cornmeal Cookies

About 4 dozen 2-inch cookies

White cornmeal is traditionally used for these rich, sandy-textured cookies, native to Mexico, because its flavor is considered more delicate—but yellow cornmeal also yields good results.

Position a rack in the center of the oven. Preheat the oven to 350°F. Grease cookie sheets.

Using an electric mixer, beat together until very fluffy and well blended:

½ pound (2 sticks) unsalted butter, softened

⅔ cup sugar

2 large egg yolks

1 ½ teaspoons vanilla

⅛ teaspoon salt

Beat in until well combined:

¾ cup white cornmeal

Stir in, then knead until well blended and smooth:

2 cups all-purpose flour

Let the dough stand for 5 minutes. Pull off small pieces of dough and roll between your palms to form scant 1-inch balls. Lightly press 1 side of each ball into:

¾ cup pinenuts or slivered blanched almonds

Space the balls, nut side up, about 1 inch apart on the cookie sheets. Gently flatten the balls into 1¾-inch rounds with the heel of your hand. Bake, 1 sheet at a time, until barely colored on top and lightly browned at the edges, 12 to 16 minutes. Rotate the sheet halfway through baking for even browning. Remove the sheet to a rack and let stand briefly. Then transfer the cookies to racks to cool completely.

Mexican Wedding Cakes ❄

About 5 dozen 1¼-inch cookies

In Mexico, where they're often served at weddings, these are known as Pastelitas de Boda, or Little Wedding Cakes. They are also known as Pecan Butter Balls.

Position a rack in the upper third of the oven. Preheat the oven to 350°F. Grease cookie sheets.

Toast, stirring occasionally, in a baking pan until lightly browned, 5 to 8 minutes:

1 cup coarsely chopped pecans

Set aside to cool completely, then grind until very finely chopped but not powdery or oily. Beat on medium speed until very fluffy and well blended:

½ pound (2 sticks) unsalted butter, softened

¼ teaspoon salt

½ cup powdered sugar

2 teaspoons vanilla

Gradually beat the pecans into the butter mixture. Sift over the top and stir in until well blended:

2 cups all-purpose flour

Pull off pieces of the dough and roll between your palms into generous 1-inch balls. Space about 1¼ inches apart on the sheets. Bake, 1 sheet at a time, until the cookies are faintly tinged with brown, 12 to 15 minutes; rotate the sheet halfway through baking for even browning. Remove the sheet to a rack and let stand until the cookies firm slightly. Transfer the cookies to racks to cool completely. Roll the cookies until coated all over in:

⅓ cup powdered sugar

Viennese Crescents ❄

About 4 dozen 2¼-inch cookies

Position a rack in the upper third of the oven. Preheat the oven to 350°F. Grease cookie sheets.

Beat on medium speed until lightened in color and creamy:

½ pound (2 sticks) unsalted butter, softened

Sift over the top and beat until well combined:

¾ cup powdered sugar

Stir in:

2 teaspoons vanilla

1 cup ground walnuts or ground blanched almonds

Gradually sift over the top while stirring:

2 cups all-purpose flour

Knead until well blended. Pull off generous 1-tablespoon pieces of the dough, roll with your hands into a short rope, and shape into crescents, shown below. (If the dough is soft and difficult to handle, refrigerate until slightly firm.) Space 1¼ inches apart on the sheets.

Bake, 1 sheet at a time, until the crescents are faintly tinged with brown and slightly darker at the edges, 13 to 16 minutes; rotate the sheet halfway through baking for even browning. Remove the sheet to a rack and let stand until the cookies firm slightly. Transfer the cookies to racks to cool. Sift over the cookies until evenly coated:

⅔ cup powdered sugar

Pfeffernüsse (Peppernuts) ❄

About 5 dozen 1-inch cookies

These cookies may firm up and even become hard during storage. To soften them slightly, add an apple slice wrapped in a paper towel to the storage container for a few days.

Whisk together thoroughly:

**1 cup plus 1 tablespoon
   all-purpose flour**
1 teaspoon ground cinnamon
½ teaspoon ground cardamom
¼ teaspoon ground cloves
¼ teaspoon ground nutmeg
⅛ teaspoon ground black pepper
¼ teaspoon baking powder
⅛ teaspoon baking soda
⅛ teaspoon salt

Beat until very fluffy:

½ cup sugar

**4 tablespoons (½ stick) unsalted
   butter, softened**

Add and beat until well combined:

1 large egg yolk

Stir in:

**¼ cup slivered blanched almonds,
   finely chopped**
**¼ cup finely chopped candied
   orange peel**
1 teaspoon finely grated lemon zest

Stir the flour mixture into the butter mixture in 3 parts, alternating with, in 2 parts:

**3 tablespoons light or dark
   molasses**
3 tablespoons brandy

Cover and refrigerate the dough for at least 8 hours or up to 2 days to

allow the flavors to blend.

To bake, position a rack in the upper third of the oven. Preheat the oven to 350°F. Grease cookie sheets. Pull off pieces of the dough and roll between your palms into scant ¾-inch balls. Space about 1 inch apart on the sheets. Bake, 1 sheet at a time, until the cookies are faintly tinged with brown on top and slightly darker at the edges, 12 to 14 minutes; rotate the sheet halfway through baking for even browning. Remove the sheet to a rack and let the cookies stand briefly. Roll the cookies until well coated in:

½ to ⅔ cup powdered sugar

Let cool completely.

Kourambiedes ❄

About 4 dozen 1¼-inch cookies

These Greek cookies (opposite) are so buttery and fine in texture that they melt in the mouth. Handle gently, as these cookies are fragile.

Beat on medium speed until lightened in color and creamy:

¾ pound (3 sticks) unsalted butter, softened

¼ teaspoon salt

Beat in until very fluffy and well blended:

⅔ cup powdered sugar

1 large egg yolk

2 tablespoons brandy

1 teaspoon vanilla

Gradually add and stir until well blended and smooth:

3 cups all-purpose flour, sifted

Cover and refrigerate the dough until firm enough to shape into balls, about 1 hour.

To bake, position a rack in the upper third of the oven. Preheat the oven to 350°F. Grease cookie sheets. Pull off pieces of the dough and roll between your palms into generous 1-inch balls. Space about 1 inch apart on the sheets. If desired, garnish the balls by inserting into the top of each:

1 whole clove

Bake, 1 sheet at a time, until the cookies are faintly tinged with brown, 14 to 18 minutes; rotate the sheet halfway through baking for even browning. Remove the sheet to a rack and let stand until the cookies firm slightly. Gently transfer the cookies to racks to cool completely. Sift over the cookies until evenly coated:

½ cup powdered sugar

Benne Seed Wafers (Sesame Seed Wafers)

About 4½ dozen 2¼-inch cookies

West African for "sesame," benne is still used all over the South. Benne Seed Wafers are so nutty tasting that people often think they contain peanuts.

Position a rack in the center of the oven. Preheat the oven to 375°F. Grease cookie sheets. Place in a large skillet over medium heat:

¾ cup hulled sesame seeds

Toast the seeds, shaking the pan every few seconds, until they just turn pale brown, 5 to 7 minutes. Remove from the heat and stir for 30 seconds. Cool completely. Whisk together thoroughly:

1½ cups all-purpose flour

1¼ teaspoons baking powder

½ teaspoon baking soda

¼ teaspoon salt

Beat on medium speed until very fluffy and well blended:

8 tablespoons (1 stick) unsalted butter, softened

¾ cup packed light brown sugar

Add and beat until well combined:

1 large egg

1½ teaspoons vanilla

Stir the flour mixture and ⅓ cup of the sesame seeds into the butter mixture until well blended. Pull off pieces of the dough and roll between your palms into 1-inch balls. Dip the top of each ball into the remaining sesame seeds to coat. Space the balls, seeded side up, about 2 inches apart on the sheets. Gently flatten the balls into 1½-inch rounds with the heel of your hand. Bake, 1 sheet at a time, until the cookies are just lightly browned at the edges, 6 to 9 minutes; rotate the sheet halfway through baking for even browning. Remove the sheet to a rack and let stand until the cookies firm slightly. Transfer the cookies to racks to cool.

SESAME SEEDS

The flavor of sesame seeds is nutty and sweet. Black seeds are more flavorful and aromatic than the white. Brown sesame seeds are unhulled white seeds. All these seeds usually are toasted before using: stir constantly in a skillet over medium heat until the white and brown seeds are barely golden and the black begin to release their fragrance. Or toast in the oven: spread on a baking pan and place in a 350°F oven for 20 minutes, stirring frequently.

Mandelbrezeln (Almond Pretzels)

About 4 dozen pretzels

A sweet trompe l'oeil of a favorite snack, these small dessert pretzels are topped with a sprinkling of crunchy sugar in playful imitation of coarse salt. Chocolate fans should try the optional chocolate coating.

Sift together:

1¾ cups all-purpose flour
⅓ cup powdered sugar
⅛ teaspoon salt

Stir in:

½ cup blanched almonds, coarsely ground

Add and mix by hand until a dough forms:

12 tablespoons (1½ sticks) cold unsalted butter, cut into small pieces

1 large egg, lightly beaten
Grated zest of 1 lemon

Divide the dough in half. Wrap each portion in plastic and refrigerate for 1½ hours.

To bake, position a rack in the center of the oven. Preheat the oven to 375°F. Grease cookie sheets, or cover with parchment paper or greased aluminum foil.

Working with 1 portion of dough at a time (keep the remainder refrigerated), roll into a log 1 inch in diameter. Cut the log into 24 pieces. Roll each piece into an 8-inch-long rope, tapered at the ends, and shape into a pretzel. Repeat with the remaining dough. Transfer the pretzels to the cookie sheets, spacing 2 inches apart, and brush with:

1 large egg, lightly beaten

Sprinkle with:

½ cup coarse sugar crystals

Omit the egg wash and coarse sugar if using chocolate coating. Bake, 1 sheet at a time, until golden, 12 to 15 minutes. Remove the pretzels to racks to cool.

To coat the pretzels with the optional chocolate coating, bake as directed and let cool. Melt chocolate as for *Florentines Cockaigne*, 32. Dip each pretzel into the chocolate. Transfer the pretzels to wax paper and let stand until the chocolate is completely set.

Cantuccini (Tuscan Almond Biscotti) ❄

About 3 dozen 3 x ½-inch biscotti

Big almond nuggets stud these crunchy cookies that Tuscans love to dip in their precious Vin Santo—a delicious and unusual wine made from semidry grapes, concentrated in flavor, often amber-colored, and usually sweet—but they're just as good dunked in milk, hot coffee, or tea. These particular biscotti, modeled after the northern Italian classic, are made from more of a thick batter than a dough. Handle it with a pastry scraper for greater ease.

Position a rack in the center of the oven. Preheat the oven to 300°F. Grease and flour a cookie sheet. Spread in a small baking pan:

2½ cups whole blanched almonds

Toast, stirring frequently, until evenly browned, 8 to 12 minutes. Let cool. Using a sharp knife, chop one-third of the almonds into very large pieces and set aside in a large bowl.

Transfer the remaining almonds to a food processor. Add:

¾ cup all-purpose flour

1½ heaping tablespoons grated lemon zest

2 heaping teaspoons grated orange zest

Process until the almonds are coarsely ground and set aside. Add to the bowl with the hand-chopped almonds and stir in:

¾ cup all-purpose flour

1 teaspoon baking powder

Combine in the food processor:

½ teaspoon salt

Pinch of freshly ground pepper

2 large eggs

2 large egg whites

2½ tablespoons light corn syrup

¾ cup sugar

2 teaspoons vanilla

Process for 5 seconds. Add the nut mixture and pulse for a few seconds, just long enough to blend—do not overmix. The dough will be a dense batter. Using a rubber spatula and a pastry scraper, scrape the dough onto the cookie sheet. Shape the dough into 2 smooth, evenly shaped logs, 16 inches long x 3 inches wide x 1 inch high. Arrange the logs about 3 inches apart.

Bake for 25 minutes. Remove the sheet to a rack. Increase the oven temperature to 325°F. When the logs are just cool enough to handle, carefully transfer to a cutting board and cut crosswise, on a slight diagonal, into ½-inch-thick slices. Lay the slices flat on the sheet.

Return to the oven and bake for 12 minutes. Turn the slices over and bake for 15 minutes more. Transfer the biscotti to racks to cool.

Classic Biscotti (Reduced Fat)

About 3 dozen 3 x ½-inch biscotti

Most plain biscotti are low in fat to begin with. These cookies (above back) have less than 2 grams each.
Position a rack in the center of the oven. Preheat the oven to 375°F. Grease a cookie sheet.
Whisk together thoroughly:

3⅓ cups all-purpose flour
2½ teaspoons baking powder
½ teaspoon salt

Beat on medium speed until well blended:

¼ cup corn or canola oil
1¼ cups sugar
2 large eggs

2 large egg whites
1 teaspoon finely grated lemon zest
½ teaspoon finely grated
  orange zest
1 teaspoon anise extract or almond
  extract
1 teaspoon vanilla

Gradually stir the flour mixture into the egg mixture until well blended and smooth. Shape the dough into 2 smooth, evenly shaped 11 x 1½-inch logs, either by wrapping each log in plastic and rolling it back and forth until smooth, or by shaping it with lightly floured

hands. Arrange the logs as far apart from each other as possible on the sheet and press to flatten slightly. Bake for 25 minutes. Remove the sheet to a rack. When the logs are just cool enough to handle, carefully transfer to a cutting board and cut crosswise, on a slight diagonal, into ½-inch-thick slices. Lay the slices flat on the sheet. Return to the oven and bake for 10 minutes. Turn the slices over and bake until lightly browned, 5 to 10 minutes more. Transfer the biscotti to racks to cool.

Chocolate-Coated Mocha Biscotti

About 3½ dozen 3 x ½-inch biscotti

If you wish to freeze these cookies (opposite front and below), coat with chocolate after thawing to room temperature.

Position a rack in the center of the oven. Preheat the oven to 350°F. Grease a cookie sheet.

Spread in separate small baking pans:

1⅓ cups whole blanched almonds
1⅓ cups whole hazelnuts

Toast, stirring occasionally, until the almonds are tinged with brown and fragrant, and the hazelnut skins are loosened, 8 to 12 minutes. Let cool, then rub the hazelnuts in a dish towel or between your palms to remove as much skin as possible. Coarsely chop the nuts.

Chop into small bits:

6 ounces bittersweet or semisweet chocolate

Whisk together thoroughly:

3 cups all-purpose flour
¼ cup unsweetened cocoa
2½ teaspoons baking powder
¼ teaspoon salt

Beat on medium speed until very fluffy and well blended:

8 tablespoons (1 stick) unsalted butter, softened
1 cup sugar

Beat in 1 at a time:

3 large eggs
1 large egg white

Add and beat until the coffee is dissolved:

1½ tablespoons light corn syrup
1 tablespoon instant coffee granules or powder
1¼ teaspoons vanilla
1¼ teaspoons almond extract (optional)

Gradually stir the flour mixture into the egg mixture until well blended and smooth. Stir in the nuts and chocolate.

Shape the dough into 2 smooth, evenly shaped 15 x 1½-inch logs either by wrapping each log in plastic and rolling it back and forth until smooth, or by shaping it with lightly floured hands. Flatten the logs slightly and arrange on the sheet as far apart as possible. Bake for 35 minutes. Remove the sheet to a rack. When the logs are just cool enough to handle, carefully transfer to a cutting board and cut crosswise, on a slight diagonal, into ½-inch-thick slices. Lay the slices flat on the sheet. Return to the oven and bake until the slices are almost firm when lightly pressed on top, 16 to 20 minutes. Transfer the biscotti to racks to cool.

To prepare for adding the optional drizzled chocolate, arrange the slices in neat rows about ½ inch apart on the cookie sheet. Melt, stirring often, in the top of a double boiler over barely simmering water:

4 ounces bittersweet or semisweet chocolate, coarsely chopped
1 tablespoon corn or canola oil

Remove the top of the double boiler from the bottom and add, off the heat:

2 ounces bittersweet or semisweet chocolate, cut into ½-ounce pieces

Stir until the melted chocolate cools to just barely warm. Remove any unmelted chocolate. Immediately spoon the chocolate into a paper cone or a pastry bag fitted with a large writing tip. If using a paper cone, 15, cut off the tip to allow a ⅛-inch-wide drizzled line. Quickly drizzle long zigzag lines back and forth until all the biscotti are decorated. Let stand, chocolate side up, in a cool room until the chocolate is completely set, about 30 minutes.

Palm Leaves

About 48 small cookies

Palm leaves (palmiers in French) usually measure about 3 inches in diameter; when they are 5 to 6 inches across, they become elephant ears. We prefer the smaller ones, as they are more apt to be caramelized all the way through. Puff pastry scraps are ideal for this recipe.

Have ready 1 or 2 unbuttered baking sheets.
Measure:

1 to 1½ cups sugar

Roll out into a 12 x 5½-inch rectangle on a lightly sugared surface:

8 ounces *Food Processor Puff Pastry,* opposite

Sprinkle about ¼ cup of the sugar over the dough and roll lightly with the rolling pin to embed the sugar. With the short edge closest to you, fold the dough into thirds, like a business letter. Turn the dough so the folded edge is on the left and the open edge is on the right (like a book about to be opened). Roll out into a 13 x 7-inch rectangle with one short edge facing you. Sprinkle about 2 tablespoons of the sugar over the dough and roll lightly with the rolling pin to embed the sugar. Fold each long side of the dough toward the center, leaving a ¼-inch space in the middle (below). Lightly brush the top of one folded side with:

1 large egg white, lightly beaten

Sprinkle the other folded side with about 1 tablespoon of the sugar. Fold the dough lengthwise in half, so that the sugared surface meets the egg white, and press the 2 halves together. Place the pastry on an unbuttered baking sheet. Cover and refrigerate the dough for at least 30 minutes, or wrap airtight and freeze until ready to use.

Position a rack in the lower third of the oven. Preheat the oven to 425°F. Butter the baking sheets generously.

If the dough is frozen, let it thaw for 5 to 10 minutes before cutting. Quickly transfer the dough to a cutting board. Spread some of the sugar in a shallow bowl. Cut the dough crosswise into ¼-inch-thick slices. Press one cut side of each slice into the sugar and place sugar side down and at least 3 inches apart on a baking sheet. If necessary, push each slice back into shape. Sprinkle sugar over the tops. If you wish, make the palm leaves in 2 batches. Bake for 5 minutes, until the cookies begin to brown around the edges. Sprinkle again with sugar. Turn each cookie over with a metal spatula and sprinkle the second side with sugar. Bake until golden brown and caramelized all over, 2 to 5 minutes longer. Watch carefully, for the cookies burn quickly. Remove to a rack and let cool completely before serving (see photo page 92).

Food Processor Puff Pastry

2¾ pounds

A modernized puff pastry recipe.
Pulse to combine in a food processor:

2⅓ cups all-purpose flour
1¼ teaspoons salt

Scatter over the flour:

5 tablespoons cold unsalted butter,
 cut into ½-inch cubes

Pulse until the mixture resembles coarse crumbs. Stir to combine:

½ cup ice water
2 tablespoons fresh lemon juice
1 large egg yolk

Drizzle the mixture over the contents of the processor. Pulse just until the dough begins to come together. Scrape the dough onto a sheet of plastic wrap and form it into a 5-inch square. Wrap the dough and refrigerate for 1 hour.
Cut into ½-inch slices and freeze for 2 minutes:

28 tablespoons (3½ sticks) unsalted
 butter

Place in a food processor:

1 cup all-purpose flour

Distribute the butter slices over the flour and pulse just until the mixture looks like fine gravel; it should not be processed to a paste. Scrape the mixture onto a sheet of plastic wrap, cover, and shape into a 6-inch square. Wrap and refrigerate while rolling out the dough.

Remove the 5-inch dough square from the refrigerator. Place it on a lightly floured surface and roll into a 13 × 8-inch rectangle, keeping one 8-inch side facing you. Brush off the excess flour. Remove the butter patty from the refrigerator, unwrap it, and center it on one half of the dough (**1**). Fold the dough over the butter, completely covering it. Press the dough together on the 3 open sides. Turn the dough so that the folded edge is on the left, with one of the sealed sides (where the dough was pressed together) on the right to change the direction of the pastry for the next roll. The dough is now ready for turns.

Roll the dough package into a 17 × 7½-inch rectangle, keeping one short side of the rectangle facing you. Slide a metal dough scraper or spatula under the bottom third of the dough and fold it up. Slide the spatula under the top third of the dough and fold it down on top of the first third, as though you were folding a business letter (**2**). This rolling and folding is called a single turn. Rotate the dough so that the folded edge is on the left and the open edge is on the right (like a book about to be opened). Roll the dough once more into a 17 × 7½-inch rectangle. This time fold the bottom end up and the top end down to meet in the center (rather than overlapping), then fold the dough in half so that the folded ends meet to make 4 layers of dough (**3**). This double fold is the second turn. Mark the dough with 2 imprints to remind yourself that you have given the dough 2 turns. Wrap the dough and refrigerate for 45 minutes. With the folded edge on the left and the open edge on the right, roll the dough out again to 17 × 7½ inches. Repeat the double fold for the third turn. Mark with 3 imprints, wrap the dough, and refrigerate for 45 minutes. Roll the dough out and repeat the double fold for the fourth turn. Mark the dough with 4 imprints, wrap, and refrigerate for at least 1 hour or up to 24 hours. The puff pastry is ready to use.

Cinnamon Sugar Sticks

About 32 sticks

Roll out into a 17 x 9-inch rectangle:

1 pound Food Processor Puff Pastry, 91

Transfer the pastry to an ungreased baking sheet. Cover and refrigerate the dough for at least 30 minutes or wrap airtight and freeze until ready to use.

If the dough is frozen, let it thaw for a few minutes before cutting. Quickly transfer the pastry to a cutting board, trim ½ inch from all the sides to make a 16 x 8-inch rectangle, and cut into two 8-inch squares. Lightly brush the squares with:

1 egg, lightly beaten

Sprinkle over 1 square:

**6 tablespoons sugar mixed with
   2 teaspoons ground cinnamon**

Roll lightly with the rolling pin to embed the sugar. Brush any sugar that clings to the rolling pin back onto the pastry. Place the second square, egg side down, on top of the sugar. Roll the sugar-filled dough into a 17 x 9-inch rectangle. Return to the baking sheet and refrigerate for 30 minutes.

Transfer the dough to a cutting board. Butter 2 cookie sheets generously. Sprinkle the top of the dough with:

1 to 2 tablespoons sugar

Roll lightly with the rolling pin to embed the sugar. Trim the pastry ½ inch all around, then cut the dough crosswise into 8 x ½-inch strips. Twist each strip by holding one end on the work surface and twisting the other end about 3 revolutions. Place the twisted strips at least 1 inch apart on the cookie sheets, pressing the ends down firmly so that they don't untwist. Refrigerate or freeze until firm while the oven preheats.

Position a rack in the lower third of the oven. Preheat the oven to 425°F. Bake the sugar sticks, 1 cookie sheet at a time, until they are light brown, 10 to 15 minutes. These cook quickly because of the sugar, so watch carefully. Remove the sheet to a rack and let cool completely before serving (above right).

Glazed Lemon Dainties (Reduced Fat)

About 3 dozen 1¾-inch cookies

Position a rack in the center of the oven. Preheat the oven to 350°F. Lightly grease 2 cookie sheets. Using a wire whisk, mix thoroughly, then set aside:

2 cups cake flour (not self-rising)
½ teaspoon cream of tartar
¼ teaspoon salt
1¼ teaspoons baking powder
⅛ teaspoon baking soda

Using an electric mixer, beat together until well blended and smooth:

3 tablespoons unsalted butter, softened
3 tablespoons corn or canola oil
1 tablespoon light corn syrup
⅓ cup sugar

Add, beating until smoothly blended:

1 large egg yolk
2 tablespoons skim milk
2 teaspoons vanilla
½ teaspoon finely grated lemon zest

Gently stir the flour mixture into the egg mixture until just blended. Divide the dough into quarters; divide each quarter into 9 equal-sized pieces of dough and roll between your palms into balls. Space about 1 inch apart on the sheets. Bake the dainties, 1 cookie sheet at a time, until the tops are just barely firm to the touch and faintly tinged with brown, 10 to 13 minutes. Remove the sheet to racks and let stand until the cookies firm slightly. Transfer the cookies to racks until cool enough to handle. Meanwhile, to prepare the glaze, stir together until smooth:

1⅓ cups powdered sugar, sifted
4 teaspoons fresh lemon juice
½ teaspoon light corn syrup
¼ teaspoon vanilla
Tiny drop of yellow food coloring (optional)

If necessary, thin the glaze with a few drops of water. Dip the tops of the warm cookies into the glaze, shaking off the excess. Return the cookies to the racks and let stand until the glaze sets, about 1 hour.

Brandied Fruitcake Drops (Reduced Fat) ❄

About 3 dozen 1½-inch cookies

These cookies (opposite front) are spicy, fragrant, and full of dried fruit. Like fruitcake itself, these are good keepers.

Thoroughly stir together in a glass or ceramic bowl:

1 cup mixed diced candied citrus peel
1 cup golden raisins
1 cup dried black currants or dark raisins
½ cup chopped candied red and green cherries
⅓ cup chopped walnuts or pecans
½ cup brandy
¼ cup water
1 teaspoon finely grated orange zest

Cover and let stand, stirring several times, for at least 8 hours and up to 24 hours at cool room temperature.

Using a wire whisk, stir together:

⅔ cup all-purpose flour
¾ teaspoon ground cinnamon
½ teaspoon ground ginger
¼ teaspoon ground nutmeg
¼ teaspoon baking powder

Using an electric mixer, beat until well blended:

3 tablespoons unsalted butter, softened
3 tablespoons packed light or dark brown sugar

Add, beating until smooth:

2 tablespoons light or dark corn syrup
2 large egg whites

Stir the flour mixture and the dried fruit mixture into the butter mixture until evenly blended. Cover and freeze the dough until firm enough to shape into balls, at least 2 hours.

(The dough can also be wrapped airtight and frozen for up to 2 weeks.)

To bake, position a rack in the center of the oven. Preheat the oven to 350°F. Coat cookie sheets with non-stick spray.

With lightly greased hands, pull off pieces of the dough and roll between your palms into 1-inch balls. Space about 1½ inches apart on the sheets. Garnish each cookie with:

1 candied cherry quarter or other bit of diced candied fruit

Bake, 1 sheet at a time, until the cookies are barely firm when gently pressed on top, 9 to 12 minutes. Remove the sheet to a rack and let stand for 2 to 3 minutes. Transfer the cookies to racks to cool. Allow to mellow 24 hours before serving.

Bourbon Balls ❄

About sixty 1-inch balls

Many of our readers don't think it's Christmas without this cherished Joy classic. Keep in mind that these cookies (opposite back) get even better as they age and, packed in a tin, make a wonderful holiday gift.

Sift together into a medium bowl:

1 cup powdered sugar
2 tablespoons unsweetened Dutch-process cocoa

Whisk together until well blended:

¼ cup bourbon
2 tablespoons light corn syrup

Stir into the cocoa mixture. Crush in a food processor or electric mixer:

2½ cups vanilla wafers

(Alternatively, put the wafers in a sealable plastic bag and crush with a rolling pin or the bottom of a heavy saucepan.) Mix with:

1 cup coarsely chopped pecans

Stir the pecan mixture into the cocoa mixture. Roll into 1-inch balls between your palms (the balls do not have to be even). Sift into a shallow bowl:

½ cup powdered sugar

Roll the bourbon balls, a few at a time, in the powdered sugar. Store at room temperature between layers of wax or parchment paper in an airtight container for up to 3 weeks.

ABOUT
FILLED
COOKIES

*F*illed cookies are time consuming to prepare, but they always give the impression of being special. The fillings might be anything from jam tucked in the indentations of thumbprint cookies to thin chocolate mints sandwiched between golden wafers.

Since there is so much variety in the shaping, handling, and baking of filled cookies, not many general rules apply. Simply follow the directions provided with each recipe.

Almond Thumbprint Cookies, 99; Linzer Hearts, 98

Drei Augen ❄

About 3 dozen 1½-inch cookies

Drei Augen *means "three eyes" in German; the "eyes" are small holes in the top cookie, revealing the jelly within.*
Beat on medium speed until very fluffy and well blended:

20 tablespoons (2½ sticks) unsalted butter, softened

⅔ cup sugar

Whisk together thoroughly:

2⅓ cups all-purpose flour

½ cup whole natural (unblanched) almonds, finely ground

1 teaspoon ground cinnamon

Stir the flour mixture into the butter mixture. Divide the dough into thirds. Place each third between 2 large sheets of wax or parchment paper. Roll out into a circle 11 inches in diameter and ⅛ inch thick, checking the underside of the dough and smoothing any creases. Keeping the paper in place, layer the rolled dough on a baking sheet and refrigerate for at least 2 hours or up to 24 hours.

To bake, position a rack in the center of the oven. Preheat the oven to 350°F. Grease cookie sheets or cover with parchment paper or greased aluminum foil.

Working with 1 portion of dough at a time (leave the remainder refrigerated), gently peel away and replace 1 sheet of the paper. (This will make it easier to lift the cookies from the paper later.) Peel away and discard the second sheet. Use a 1½-inch cutter to cut out rounds, then use the small end of a ⅜-inch plain pastry tip or a drinking straw to cut out 3 small holes in half of the rounds. With a spatula, transfer the cookies to the sheets, spacing 1½ inches apart and baking the top and bottom cookies separately, as the cookies with holes bake faster. Bake, 1 sheet at a time, until the cookies are pale golden, 10 to 15 minutes. Remove the sheet to a rack and let stand until the cookies firm slightly. Transfer the cookies to racks to cool completely. Sift over the cookies with holes:

1 cup powdered sugar

Boil for 2 minutes:

1 cup red currant jelly

Cool to lukewarm. Turn over the solid cookies so the bottom side is up. Spoon ¼ teaspoon of the cooled jelly onto each cookie, then top with a cutout cookie. Press lightly so the jelly fills in the 3 holes.

LINZER HEARTS

You can also use a round cookie cutter for these favorites.
Prepare *Drei Augen, above,* omitting the holes and using a heart-shaped cutter and substituting seedless raspberry preserves for the red currant jelly.

Almond Thumbprint Cookies (Reduced Fat) ❄

About 3½ dozen 1¾-inch cookies

These cookies contain only about 2 grams of fat apiece and are festive enough for a tea table. Be sure to use thick seedless jam or preserves, not jelly, so the filling will not be runny.

Position a rack in the center of the oven. Preheat the oven to 375°F. Grease cookie sheets.

Whisk together thoroughly:

1½ cups all-purpose flour
⅓ cup cornstarch
¼ teaspoon baking powder
¼ teaspoon baking soda
¼ teaspoon salt

Beat on medium speed until well blended:

3½ tablespoons unsalted butter, softened

3 tablespoons corn or canola oil
1 tablespoon light corn syrup
½ cup sugar
1 large egg
¼ teaspoon very finely grated lemon zest
2½ teaspoons vanilla
¼ teaspoon almond extract

Stir the flour mixture into the egg mixture just until combined. With lightly greased hands, pull off pieces of the dough and roll between your palms into ¾-inch balls. Do not make them larger, as the cookies should be small and will puff and spread a bit during baking. Space the balls about 2 inches apart on the sheets. With your thumb or knuckle,

press down the center of each ball to make a large, deep well. Fill the wells with:

About ⅔ cup seedless fruit jam or preserves, such as cherry, apricot, damson plum, or raspberry

Very lightly sprinkle the tops of the cookies with:

2 to 3 tablespoons chopped sliced blanched or natural (unblanched) almonds

Bake, 1 sheet at a time, until the tops are just barely tinged with brown, 6 to 9 minutes. Remove the sheet to a rack and let stand until the cookies firm slightly, about 2 minutes. Transfer the cookies to racks to cool.

Austrian Wreaths ❋

About 2 dozen cookies

Grease cookie sheets or cover with parchment paper or greased aluminum foil.
Sift into a bowl:

⅔ cup powdered sugar

Add and beat until lightened in color and creamy:

15 tablespoons unsalted butter, softened

Add:

1 large egg yolk

Sift together:

1¾ cups all-purpose flour

¼ teaspoon ground cloves

¼ teaspoon ground cinnamon

Stir the flour mixture into the butter mixture until well blended and smooth.
Stir in:

¾ cup blanched almonds, finely ground

Wrap the dough in plastic and refrigerate for 1½ hours.
Divide the dough into quarters. Place each quarter between 2 large sheets of wax or parchment paper. Roll out ⅛ inch thick, checking the underside of the dough and smoothing any creases. Working with 1 portion of dough at a time, gently peel away and replace 1 sheet of the paper. (This will make it easier to lift the cookies from the paper later.) Peel away and discard the second sheet. Use a 2½-inch cutter to cut out rounds, then use a 1½-inch cutter to cut out the centers from half of the rounds, forming rings. Roll the dough scraps, cutting out equal numbers of rounds and rings. Arrange the shapes on separate cookie sheets and refrigerate for 1 hour.

To bake, preheat the oven to 350°F. Spread on a plate:

1 cup sliced almonds

Brush 1 side of the rings with:

1 large egg white, lightly beaten

Press the glazed side of each ring into the nuts, then return to the sheet. Bake, 1 sheet at a time, until lightly browned, 10 to 12 minutes for the rings, and 10 to 15 minutes for the rounds. Let stand until the cookies firm slightly. Transfer the cookies to racks to cool. Spread the rounds with:

½ cup apricot jam, heated and strained

Top each with an almond-coated ring, pressing down lightly.

Pecan Tassies

About 2 dozen 2-inch tassies

Reminiscent of pecan pie, these tartlets are a snap to make. The recipe calls for inexpensive mini muffin pans. If you have individual tartlet pans, they would be even better here.

Finely chop in a food processor with on/off pulses:

1 cup pecan halves

Remove the nuts to a medium bowl and set aside.

Combine in the food processor:

1⅓ cups all-purpose flour
⅓ cup powdered sugar
¼ teaspoon salt

Process with on/off pulses for about 5 seconds.

Sprinkle over the flour mixture:

10 tablespoons (1¼ sticks) cold unsalted butter, cut into small pieces

Process with on/off pulses until the mixture resembles coarse meal, about 20 seconds. Add, while processing with on/off pulses:

4 teaspoons ice water

Process until the dough just holds together; if necessary, add a bit more water, but do not overmoisten or overprocess.

(Alternatively, if a processor is unavailable, chop the pecans by hand and set aside. Mix the flour and powdered sugar together. Sprinkle the butter over the top. Using a pastry blender, 2 knives, or your fingertips, cut the butter into the flour until the mixture resembles coarse meal. Sprinkle water over the top, tossing with a fork. Mix until the dough just holds together, adding a bit more water if necessary, but being careful not to overmoisten.)

Press the dough into a ball. Wrap in plastic and refrigerate for 10 to 15 minutes.

To bake, position a rack in the upper third of the oven. Preheat the oven to 375°F. Generously coat two 12-muffin mini muffin pans or 24 individual tartlet pans with non-stick spray.

Add to the reserved chopped pecans and beat with a fork until well blended:

¼ cup packed light brown sugar
⅓ cup dark corn syrup
1 large egg
1 tablespoon unsalted butter, melted
1 teaspoon vanilla

Divide the dough in half. Divide each half into 12 equal portions and roll between your palms into smooth balls. Place the balls in the muffin cups or tartlet pans. With your thumb or knuckle, form a deep well in the center of each ball. Press the dough upward from the bottom and sides so it reaches the rim of the pan all the way around, being careful not to break through the dough. Spoon the nut mixture into each indentation to completely fill it. Place the muffin or tartlet pans on a cookie sheet.

Bake until the edges are browned and the filling is puffed and set, 22 to 27 minutes. (The filling will sink slightly as the tassies cool.) Remove the muffin or tartlet pans to racks and let stand until the tassies have contracted from the sides of the pan and can be easily removed. Transfer the tassies to racks to cool.

Gazelle's Horns ❄

About 2½ dozen cookies

Here is a bite-sized version of the best-loved pastry in Morocco, also good for the vegans in the family.

Whisk together thoroughly:

2 cups all-purpose flour

⅛ teaspoon salt

Stir in until a rough dough is formed:

½ cup water

¼ cup orange flower water or orange juice

3 tablespoons olive or canola oil

Knead for 5 minutes, until smooth and elastic. Wrap in plastic and refrigerate for at least 1 hour.

Whisk together thoroughly:

1⅓ cups almonds, finely ground

½ cup sugar

½ teaspoon ground cinnamon

1 tablespoon grated orange zest

Stir in until a smooth paste is formed:

2 to 3 tablespoons orange flower water or orange juice

To bake, preheat the oven to 350°F. Cover cookie sheets with parchment paper.

On a lightly floured work surface, roll the dough into a 16 x 18-inch rectangle. Cut into six 16 x 3-inch strips. Shape 1½ teaspoons of the almond mixture into logs 1½ inches long. Evenly space 5 logs, end to end, along each strip of dough.

Brush the dough lightly with water, then fold it over the almond logs, and press gently to seal. Using a pastry wheel, cut half-moon shapes around the cookies, beginning and ending at the folded edge. Gently bend each cookie into a crescent shape and prick the top with the tines of a fork.

Bake until very lightly colored, 20 to 25 minutes. Remove the sheets to wire racks and let stand until the cookies firm slightly. Transfer the cookies to racks to cool. When completely cool, sift over the cookies:

½ cup powdered sugar

Chocolate Mint Surprises

About 2½ dozen 2¼-inch cookies

In contrast to most sandwich cookies, which are assembled after the wafers are completely cool, these must be put together while the cookies are still hot from the oven, so the chocolate will melt and stick to the cookie layers.

Place in a large bowl:

½ pound (2 sticks) unsalted butter, chilled but not firm and cut into small pieces

2¼ cups all-purpose flour

Using a pastry blender, 2 knives, or your fingertips, cut in the butter until the mixture resembles fine crumbs.

Beat together with a fork until well blended:

2 large egg yolks

¾ cup sugar

¼ teaspoon salt

1 teaspoon vanilla

Stir the egg yolk mixture into the flour mixture, then knead to form a smooth dough. Divide the dough in half. Place each half between 2 large sheets of wax or parchment paper.

Roll out to a generous ⅛ inch thick, checking the underside of the dough and smoothing any creases. Keeping the paper in place, layer the rolled dough on a baking sheet and freeze until cold and slightly firm, about 20 minutes.

Position a rack in the upper third of the oven. Preheat the oven to 350°F. Grease cookie sheets.

Working with 1 portion of dough at a time (leave the other in the freezer), gently peel away and replace 1 sheet of the paper. (This will make it easier to lift the cookies from the paper later.) Peel away and discard the second sheet.

Cut out the cookies using a fluted or plain round 2¼-inch cutter (or the rim of a small glass), or cut to a size just large enough that the thin mint candies will fit within them. With a spatula, transfer the cookies to the sheets, spacing about 1 inch apart. Roll any dough scraps between the paper and continue cutting out cookies until all the dough is used; if the dough becomes too warm to handle, chill it again briefly. Bake, 1 sheet at a time, just until the cookies are lightly colored on top and slightly darker at the edges, 9 to 14 minutes. Rotate the sheet halfway through baking for even browning. Remove the sheet to a rack and let the cookies stand just until firm enough to lift but still hot. Turn half of the cookies bottom up on the cookie sheet. Immediately cover each bottom with:

1 thin square chocolate mint wafer (about 30 total)

Cover with the cookie tops, top side up, and press down lightly. Let the sandwiches stand on the cookie sheets until the mints melt. Transfer the sandwiches to racks and let stand until the cookies are cool and the filling is set; during the cooling process, adjust any sandwiches that slip askew.

Rugelach

About 30 rectangular rugelach or 24 large or 48 small crescents

Beat on medium speed until well blended, 15 to 20 seconds:

½ pound (2 sticks) unsalted butter, softened

6 ounces cream cheese, softened

Add all at once and beat on low speed just until the dough comes together, 10 to 15 seconds:

2¼ cups all-purpose flour

Divide the dough into thirds. Flatten each third into a 6 x 4-inch rectangle or 6-inch circle for crescents. Wrap in plastic and refrigerate for 1 hour.

To bake, position a rack in the upper third of the oven. Preheat the oven to 350°F. Cover a cookie sheet with parchment paper.

Whisk together:

⅓ cup sugar

1 teaspoon ground cinnamon

Working quickly with 1 portion of dough at a time (leave the remainder refrigerated), generously sprinkle the work surface and the top of the dough with all-purpose flour.

FOR RECTANGULAR RUGELACH:

Shape by rolling each portion into a 16 x 10-inch rectangle, about ⅛ inch thick. Brush the excess flour from the top and bottom of the dough, and the work surface, and turn the rectangle so the long edge is parallel to the edge of the work surface. Leaving a ¼-inch border, spread 1 rectangle with:

¼ cup raspberry jam or apricot preserves (not jelly)

Along the edge of the jam on the long side nearest you, place a line of:

¼ cup raisins or chocolate chips

Sprinkle the rest of the surface with 2 teaspoons of the cinnamon and sugar and:

2½ tablespoons ground walnuts

Roll the dough, starting at the raisin edge, gently tucking and tightening as you go.

Finish with the seam of the roll facing down. Cut the roll into 1½-inch-thick slices. Repeat with the remaining rectangles.

FOR CRESCENT RUGELACH:

Shape by rolling each portion into a circle about 14 inches in diameter and about ⅛ inch thick. Spread the jam in a thin layer, leaving a ¼-inch border, then sprinkle the entire surface with the raisins, cinnamon sugar, and ground nuts. Cut the circle like a pizza, creating 8 (for large cookies) or 16 (for small cookies) even triangles. Roll up from the wide end to the point, tucking the point under. Repeat with the remaining circles.

TO BAKE RUGELACH:

With a spatula, transfer the rugelach to the cookie sheet. Sprinkle each cookie with ⅛ teasooon of the cinnamon sugar. Bake until the bottoms are light golden (the tops will still be blond), about 25 minutes. Remove the sheet to a rack and let stand until the rugelach firm slightly. Transfer the rugelach to racks to cool.

Cranberry Cherry Pinwheels (Reduced Fat) ❄

About 6 dozen 2¾-inch cookies

Made with lightly sweetened, dried cranberries and cherry preserves, these are colorful cookies with a crisp-chewy texture and zesty fruit taste. They are also extremely convenient, since the pinwheel logs may be kept in the freezer for several weeks. Slicing and baking the cookies takes only a few minutes.

Combine in a medium saucepan:

**1½ cups sweetened dried
   cranberries**
1 cup cherry preserves
¼ cup water
½ teaspoon ground cinnamon

Simmer, stirring frequently, until the mixture is soft and most of the liquid is absorbed, 5 to 8 minutes. If the mixture is dry, stir in a bit more water. Remove to a food processor and process until smooth. Cover and refrigerate until cool. (The filling can be stored in the refrigerator for up to 2 days. Return to room temperature and stir well before using.) Whisk together thoroughly and set aside:

3⅓ cups all-purpose flour
¾ teaspoon baking powder
½ teaspoon salt
½ teaspoon ground cinnamon
⅛ teaspoon baking soda

Beat on medium speed until well combined:

1¼ cups sugar
**4 tablespoons (½ stick) unsalted
   butter, softened**
3 tablespoons corn or canola oil
3 large egg whites
2 tablespoons milk
2 teaspoons vanilla
**1½ teaspoons finely grated
   orange zest**

Beat in half of the flour mixture until just combined, then stir in the remainder until well blended. Divide the dough in half. Form each half into a log about 6 inches long. Place each log between 2 large sheets of wax or parchment paper. Press, then roll each log into an 11-inch square, checking the underside of the dough and smoothing any creases. Patch the dough as necessary to make the sides relatively straight. Keeping the paper in place, layer the rolled dough on a baking sheet and refrigerate until cold and slightly firm, about 30 minutes. Working with 1 square of dough at a time (leave the other refrigerated), gently peel away and discard the top sheet of paper. Spread half of the filling in a thin, even layer over the entire surface of the dough. Tightly roll up the dough jelly-roll style, peeling away the second sheet of paper as you roll.

Wrap each roll in wax paper, twisting the ends of the paper to prevent unrolling. Place on a baking sheet and freeze until the rolls are firm enough to be cut neatly, about 2½ hours. Use immediately or transfer to sealable plastic bags and freeze for up to 1 month.

To bake, position a rack in the upper third of the oven. Preheat the oven to 375°F. Generously coat several cookie sheets with nonstick spray. Gently unwrap the rolls and cut crosswise into scant ¼-inch-thick slices. Transfer the slices to the cookie sheets, spacing about 1½ inches apart. Bake until the edges are browned and the tops are lightly colored, 10 to 13 minutes. Rotate the sheets halfway through baking for even browning. Using a spatula, immediately remove the cookies to racks and let stand until cool.

ABOUT
SLICED, PIPED & PRESSED
COOKIES

What Granny Rom first called "icebox cookies" in the 1931 Joy, and Mom renamed "refrigerator cookies" in the '50s, might most accurately be called "freezer cookies" today, since the freezer is where we now store logs of slice-and-bake dough. But we've gone back to Granny Rom's term, because it brings to mind a bygone era.

Icebox cookies are convenient: The dough can be mixed when you have a few minutes, then formed into logs and stashed in the freezer (some for as long as 2 months) until you're ready to bake. There's little shaping time required, since the logs are simply cut crosswise into slices. Most kinds do not even have to be thawed before slicing—and actually slice best when very, very cold.

A pastry bag and piping tube can be used to shape a large variety of piped cookies. The dough simply needs to be soft enough to flow through the tip easily. Piped Spritz cookies, as well as a number of meringue cookies, can quickly be formed in this way.

The distinguishing feature of pressed and molded cookies is that they are shaped with molds, presses, or other special equipment not generally on hand in the kitchen. Each type of shaping device lends a different, distinctive, and decidedly handsome look.

Chocolate Chip Icebox Cookies, 110; Icebox Sugar Cookies, 110

Icebox Sugar Cookies ❄

About 3½ dozen 2½-inch cookies

These slice-and-bake logs are a cinch to make. The kids will have a field day decorating them.

Whisk together thoroughly:

1½ cups all-purpose flour
1½ teaspoons baking powder
¼ teaspoon salt

Beat on medium speed until very fluffy and well blended:

10 tablespoons (1¼ sticks)
**   unsalted butter, softened**
⅔ cup sugar

Add and beat until well combined:

1 large egg
2 teaspoons vanilla
¼ teaspoon finely grated lemon
**   zest (optional)**

Stir the flour mixture into the butter mixture until well blended and smooth. Cover and refrigerate until slightly firm, 20 to 30 minutes. Place the dough on one end of a long sheet of wax or parchment paper. With lightly greased hands, shape into an even, 11-inch-long log. Roll up in the paper, twisting the ends of the paper to prevent unrolling. Place on a baking sheet and freeze until completely frozen, at least 3 hours. Use immediately or transfer to a sealable plastic bag and freeze for up to 1 month. To bake, position a rack in the upper third of the oven. Preheat the oven to 375°F. Grease cookie sheets. Gently peel the paper off the log and cut the log crosswise into ⅛-inch-thick slices. Transfer the slices to the cookie sheets, spacing about 2 inches apart. Bake, 1 sheet at a time, until the cookies are golden all over and just slightly darker at the edges, 7 to 10 minutes. The longer the baking time, the crisper the cookies. Remove the sheet to a rack and let stand until the cookies firm slightly. Transfer the cookies to racks to cool.

CHOCOLATE CHIP ICEBOX COOKIES

3½ to 4 dozen 2½-inch cookies
We know that busy people think mixes and storebought refrigerator doughs save time. If you and your family are used to commercial mixes and doughs, you'll find home-baked cookies a revelation and reward. To our minds, the matchless flavor of real home-baked cookies more than compensates for the extra five or ten minutes spent making them. Start by mastering a few simple bar cookies and you'll soon venture even further.
Prepare *Icebox Sugar Cookies, left,* omitting the lemon zest and substituting ⅓ cup packed light brown sugar for ⅓ cup of the sugar. Add 1 cup miniature semisweet chocolate chips along with the dry ingredients.

Cream Cheese Icebox Cookies

About 3½ dozen 2¼-inch cookies

This is an easy-to-handle dough that produces a cookie with outstanding flavor.
Whisk together thoroughly:

2 cups all-purpose flour
½ teaspoon salt
½ teaspoon baking powder
⅛ teaspoon baking soda

Beat on medium speed until very fluffy and well blended:

11 tablespoons unsalted butter, softened
1 cup sugar
1 large egg

Gradually beat in until very well combined:

3 ounces cream cheese, softened and cut into chunks
1 teaspoon vanilla

¼ teaspoon finely grated lemon zest (optional)

Stir the flour mixture into the butter mixture until well blended and smooth. Refrigerate until slightly firm, about 1 hour. Place the dough on one end of a long sheet of wax or parchment paper. With well-greased hands, shape into a 12 x 2-inch log. Roll the dough up in the paper, twisting the ends of the paper to prevent unrolling. Place on a tray or baking sheet and freeze until completely frozen, at least 3 hours. Use immediately or transfer to a sealable plastic bag and freeze for up to 1 month.

To bake, position a rack in the upper third of the oven. Preheat the oven to 375°F. Grease cookie sheets. Gently peel the paper off the log and cut the log crosswise into ⅛-inch-thick slices. Transfer the slices to the cookie sheets, spacing about 2 inches apart. Using stencils or tiny cutters as a design outline, sprinkle the tops with:

Colored sugar, cinnamon and sugar, or nonpareils

Press lightly to secure nonpareils in place. Bake, 1 sheet at a time, until the cookies are tinged with brown at the edges, 7 to 11 minutes. Remove the sheet to a rack and let stand until the cookies firm slightly. Transfer the cookies to racks to cool.

Two Moons

About 6 dozen cookies

*Two elegant cookies from one recipe!
The secret is a divided dough: one half
takes pecans, the other chocolate.*

Beat together on medium speed
until very fluffy and well blended:

**15 tablespoons unsalted butter,
 softened**

⅔ cup sugar

Add and beat until well combined:

1 large egg, lightly beaten

Gradually add, ¼ cup at a time:

2½ cups all-purpose flour

Beat on low speed until well
blended and smooth.

Divide the dough in half. Wrap
1 portion in plastic and refrigerate
for 30 minutes. Divide the
remaining dough in half. Knead into
1 portion of the dough:

⅓ cup finely chopped pecans

Knead into the second portion of
dough:

**1½ ounces finely chopped bitter-
 sweet or semisweet chocolate**

Roll each flavored dough into a
10-inch-long log and set aside.
On a lightly floured work surface,
roll the chilled dough into an 11 x
9-inch rectangle, and cut it in half
lengthwise. Brush with:

1 large egg, lightly beaten

Place 1 flavored log in the center of
each long rectangle. Completely
wrap each log with the dough,
gently smoothing the seams at the
bottom and ends. Brush with:

1 large egg, lightly beaten

Roll in:

½ cup coarse sugar crystals

Wrap in plastic and refrigerate for at
least 4 hours.

To bake, preheat the oven to 400°F.
Cover cookie sheets with parchment
paper or greased aluminum foil.
Slice each roll into 36 cookies and
place on the sheets. Bake until
golden brown, about 10 minutes.
Remove the cookies to racks to cool.

Gingerbread House ❄

One 8-inch-wide x 9-inch-tall house

Although gingerbread houses are associated with Christmas, you can create a gingerbread Easter bunny hutch or Halloween witch's cottage just by changing the decorations in this recipe.

GINGERBREAD DOUGH:

Whisk together thoroughly:

6 cups all-purpose flour
½ teaspoon baking powder
4 teaspoons ground ginger
4 teaspoons ground cinnamon
½ teaspoon ground cloves or
   allspice
½ teaspoon salt

Beat on medium speed until very fluffy and well blended:

12 tablespoons (1½ sticks)
   unsalted butter, softened
1½ cups packed light brown sugar

Beat in until well combined:

2 large eggs
1 cup dark molasses
1 tablespoon water

Beat half of the flour mixture into the molasses mixture until well blended and smooth. Stir in the remaining flour, then knead the mixture until well blended. If the dough is soft, stir in more flour until it is firmer and more manageable but not at all dry.

Place the dough in a sealable plastic bag or airtight plastic container. Set aside in a cool place, but not the refrigerator, for at least 2 hours or up to 6 hours. Or refrigerate the dough for up to 3 days; bring to room temperature before using.

CUTTING OUT PATTERN PIECES:

Meanwhile, cut out pattern pieces using paper thin enough to see through, but heavy enough not to wrinkle easily. The template pieces shown on pages 116 and 117 are drawn to actual size. (See also *Making a Template*, 61.) Trace them onto your paper, then cut out and label the pattern pieces as follows:

One piece for the front and back
   of the house (5½ inches wide
   x 7½ inches high)
One piece for the roof (7 inches
   wide x 6½ inches high)
One piece for the sides of the house
   (5 inches wide x 3 inches high)

For the chimney, cut out the pieces as follows:

One piece for the chimney front
   (1 inch wide x 3 inches high)
One piece for the chimney back
   (1 inch wide x 1½ inches high)
One piece for the chimney sides
   (1 inch wide and 2¾ inches high
   on one side and 1½ inches high
   on the other)

ROLLING OUT THE DOUGH:

Position a rack in the center of the oven. Preheat the oven to 350°F. Have ready several cookie sheets. Divide the dough in half. Working with 1 portion at a time (leave the other covered to prevent drying), roll out the dough to a scant ¼ inch thick directly on a large sheet of wax or parchment paper; keep the layer as uniform as possible. This is easier if you have a set of ¼-inch dowels to lay on all 4 sides of the dough and to use as guides, but these are not essential. Lightly dust the rolling pin with flour to prevent sticking.

CUTTING OUT THE HOUSE PIECES:

Before placing pattern pieces on the dough, lightly rub the surface of the dough with a small amount of flour. Gently lay as many pattern pieces as will fit on the dough. Using a sharp knife, wiping the blade clean as you work, cut out the following pieces (**1**): house front, back, 2 roofs, and 2 sides. Cut away the front door opening, reserving the door piece. If desired, also cut away the centered upstairs window; then split the cutout piece in half lengthwise to use as shutters. Also cut out the chimney front, back, and 2 side pieces. Immediately lift the patterns from the surface of the dough to prevent sticking. Peel away the excess dough from around the cutout pieces and reserve the scraps in a sealable plastic bag to prevent drying. As necessary, cut apart the parchment paper with scissors so individual house pieces (along with the paper) can be transferred to the cookie sheets; group large house pieces together on larger cookie sheets, and chimney, door, and shutter pieces, if using, together on a smaller sheet, spacing the pieces about 1 inch apart.

If wax or parchment paper is unavailable, roll the dough out on a lightly floured work surface, lifting the dough frequently and lightly dusting the rolling pin with flour as needed to prevent sticking. Using a wide thin-bladed spatula, gently transfer the pieces from the work surface to lightly greased cookie sheets, trying not to stretch them out of shape. If pieces do stretch, trim them back to the original pattern size using a paring knife; remove the scraps from the cookie sheets. Reserve all the scraps in a sealable plastic bag.

Continue rolling out the dough and cutting out until all the pieces are prepared. If desired, add a curved roof tile design to the roof pieces by pressing the curve of a flatware spoon into the dough surface to produce indentations at regular intervals. If desired, add clapboard texture to the house sides, front, and back, by drawing the back of a fork horizontally across the dough surface so the tines produce lines.

BAKING THE HOUSE PIECES:
Bake just until the pieces are tinged with brown and beginning to darken at the edges, 11 to 15 minutes for larger house pieces, 6 to 8 minutes for chimney, door, and shutter pieces; rotate the sheets halfway through baking for even browning. Remove the sheets to racks and let stand until the pieces are cool and firm, about 15 minutes. Transfer the pieces, along with the parchment paper, to racks to cool.

CONSTRUCTING THE HOUSE:
Royal Icing, 12, is the glue for constructing your gingerbread house. Double the recipe to yield enough for both gluing and decorating the finished house with "snow" or other finishing piping.
If you have a pastry bag and large writing tip, apply the icing glue with it. Otherwise, apply it as neatly as possible using a spoon or the tip of a knife. Working on a large wax- or parchment-paper-lined tray, start by putting the house front, sides, and back together. Pipe a line of icing on each end of 1 side piece. Place it between the front and back

pieces, gently pressing at the joints to lightly hold it in place until the second side is added. Add icing to the second side piece and fit it in place between the front and back, adjusting as necessary to make the house square. Working on 1 side of the house at a time, pipe icing along the angled front (**2**) and back edges. Grasp 1 roof piece by the edges and lay it against the piped edges, gently pressing to lightly hold it in place until the second roof piece is added. To finish the roof, pipe icing along the angled front and back edges as well as the top edge of the roof piece already in place. Press the second piece in place, adjusting so it fits snugly against the first roof piece to form a peak. Force additional icing into any seams that need reinforcing, wiping off the excess with your fingertip.
For the chimney, glue the 4 pieces together as for the house base. Before icing the base, set the chimney in place on the rooftop. If it does not sit up straight, carefully

trim the chimney bottom with a sharp knife until the bottom angle aligns evenly with the rooftop. Then pipe icing on the base of the chimney and secure it in place on the rooftop. Let the house stand, uncovered, for at least 1 hour and preferably for 8 hours before decorating.

DECORATING THE HOUSE:
Decorate according to the season. For Christmas, you may want to add Royal Icing, 12, snow and icicles along the edges of the roof (**3**), and accent the house with candy canes, peppermint pinwheels (**4**), and other appropriate sweets. For an Easter bunny hutch, snow should be omitted and replaced by pastel-tinted icing to cover seams and to accent roof lines. Candies could include miniature eggs, jelly beans, Jordan almonds, and tiny chocolate bunnies. A Halloween cottage might feature harvest colors, a shredded wheat thatched roof and seasonal goodies such as tiny pumpkin-shaped candies, licorice sticks, and candy corn.

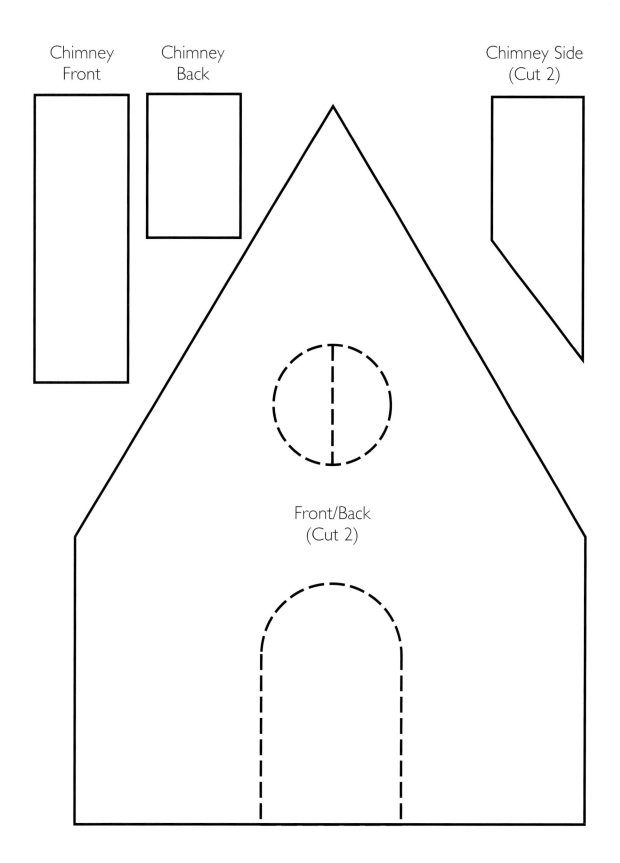

Chimney Front

Chimney Back

Chimney Side (Cut 2)

Front/Back (Cut 2)

Coffee Snaps

About 4 dozen cookies

The secret to this cookie is instant espresso powder mellowed with Kahlúa. Shaped into a log, the dough slices like a dream and freezes beautifully for up to 4 weeks.

Stir together in a small bowl:

4 teaspoons Kahlúa

2 teaspoons instant espresso powder

Whisk together thoroughly:

2½ cups all-purpose flour

¼ teaspoon ground cinnamon

⅛ teaspoon salt

Beat on medium speed until well blended and no lumps of sugar remain:

½ pound (2 sticks) unsalted butter, softened

¾ cup packed dark brown sugar

Add the espresso mixture and beat until blended. Gradually add the flour mixture, beating on low speed until blended and beginning to form a dough. Place the dough on a large piece of plastic wrap. Using the plastic wrap to help mold the dough, shape it into a 12 x 3 x 1-inch log. Wrap tightly in plastic and refrigerate until very firm, about 6 hours. Use immediately or transfer to a sealable plastic bag and freeze for up to 1 month.

To bake, position a rack in the upper third of the oven. Preheat the oven to 350°F. Line cookie sheets with parchment paper.

Gently unwrap the log and cut crosswise into ⅜-inch-thick slices. Transfer the slices to the cookie sheets, spacing about 1 inch apart. Bake, 1 sheet at a time, until the tops look dry and slightly brown around the edges, about 12 minutes. Remove the sheet to a rack and let stand until the cookies firm slightly. Transfer the cookies to racks to cool completely.

Madeleines

About 2 dozen teacakes

*These buttery French teacakes, some-
thing between a sponge cake and a
butter cake in texture, are traditionally
baked in scallop-shaped madeleine
molds, but you can use miniature
muffin pans or small tartlet pans in
any shape.*

Have all ingredients at room temperature, 68° to 70°F. Preheat the oven
to 450°F. Using melted butter, generously grease 2 madeleine pans,
each with 12 molds.

Sift together and return to the sifter:

1½ cups sifted cake flour
½ teaspoon baking powder
¼ teaspoon salt

In a medium bowl, mash and beat
with a wooden spoon or rubber
spatula until very soft and creamy:

12 tablespoons (1½ sticks) unsalted
**   butter, cut into small pieces**

Warm the bowl by dipping it into
hot water if necessary to hasten the
softening of the butter. In a large
bowl, beat on high speed until thick
and pale yellow, about 2 minutes:

3 large eggs
1 large egg yolk
¾ cup sugar
1½ teaspoons vanilla

Sift the flour mixture over the top
and fold in with a rubber spatula.
Fold a dollop of the egg mixture
into the butter. Scrape the butter

mixture back into the remaining egg
mixture and fold together. Let rest
for at least 30 minutes.

Fill the molds three-quarters full; set
any remaining batter aside. Bake
until the cakes are golden on the top
and golden brown around the
edges, 8 to 10 minutes. Immediately
loosen each cake with the tip of a
slim knife and unmold onto a rack
to cool. If necessary, wipe the molds
clean, let cool, rebutter them, and
repeat the baking process with the
remaining batter. These are best the
day they are made, but they can be
stored in an airtight container for a
day or two.

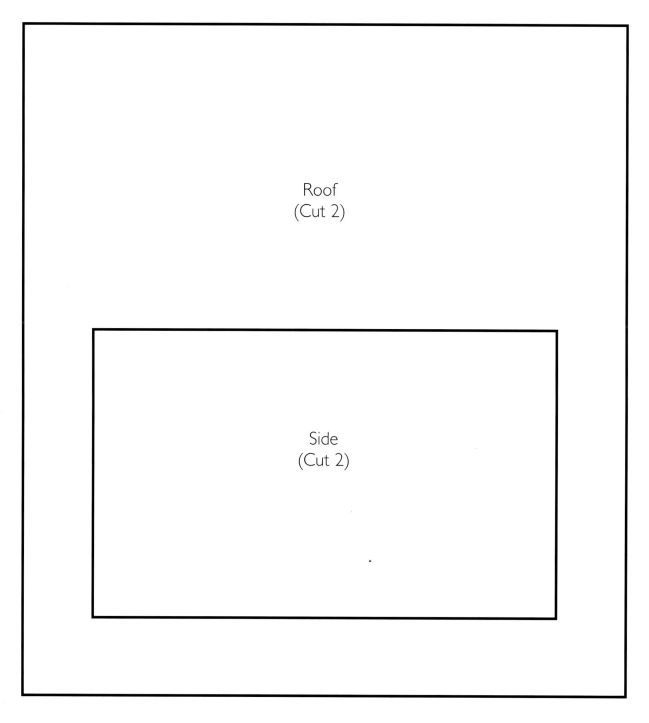

Roof
(Cut 2)

Side
(Cut 2)

Cut side pieces of house separately from roof pieces.

Spekulatius ❋

1 to 2 dozen cookies depending on size of molds

A Christmas specialty from the Rhineland, these cookies are also a favorite in Holland, where they are called speculaas and are sometimes made into figures as tall as 2 feet for the Feast of Saint Nicholas. Unlike Springerle molds, 124, which imprint designs on the dough, Spekulatius molds serve as forms for it: a portion of the dough is pushed into the carved-out indentation; the mold is then rapped on the counter to release the dough. If you don't have Spekulatius molds, use ceramic cookie molds stocked by most kitchen stores at Christmastime.

Whisk together thoroughly:

2¾ cups all-purpose flour
1 tablespoon ground cinnamon
1¼ teaspoons ground allspice
¼ teaspoon ground nutmeg

Beat on medium speed until well blended:

12 tablespoons (1½ sticks)
   unsalted butter, softened
1¼ cups packed dark brown sugar
1 large egg
1 tablespoon milk
2 teaspoons vanilla
¼ teaspoon almond extract
½ teaspoon finely grated
   lemon zest

Stir in the flour mixture until well blended and smooth. Wrap the dough in plastic and refrigerate for at least 8 hours or up to 3 days. (The dough can also be frozen for up to 1 month. Thaw it completely in the refrigerator before using.) To bake, position a rack in the center of the oven. Preheat the oven to 350°F. Grease cookie sheets. Prepare the molds by lightly brushing vegetable oil over all the interior surfaces, being sure to reach all the crevices and indentations. Lightly sprinkle or sift flour over the molds, tipping the molds back and forth until all the crevices are coated. Tap out all the excess flour. The molds must be dusted with flour after each cookie, but they do not need to be reoiled. Working with a small portion of the dough at a time (leave the remainder refrigerated), pull off pieces large enough to fill the mold, and press the dough into the form. Even if the dough seems too stiff at first, work with it; it will soften as the cookie is formed. When the interior is completely filled, press down all over to remove air pockets. Push any dough protruding over the edges back inside the edges of the mold. Cut away the excess dough so the cookie is flush with the back of the mold.

To remove the cookie from a wooden mold, hold the mold upside down and rap it repeatedly and sharply against a hard surface until the cookie loosens. For a ceramic mold, rap it a little more gently against a wooden board or other slightly softer surface to avoid chipping or breaking the form. When the cookie is loosened all over, tap or peel it out onto the sheet. If one particular section sticks, very carefully loosen it with the point of a knife. Space the cookies about 1½ inches apart. Bake, 1 sheet at a time, until the cookies are tinged with brown at the edges, 15 to 25 minutes. Remove the sheet to a rack and let stand until the cookies firm slightly. Transfer the cookies to racks to cool.

Piped and Pressed Spritz Cookies ❄

About 5 dozen 2-inch cookies

No self-respecting Scandinavian baker is ever without a supply of Spritz dough in the refrigerator. Both piping and pressing work with this dough. For those who have never formed cookies with either method, piping is likely to yield better results with less practice. In fact, most cooks can turn out rosettes and stars that look as fancy as store-bought on the first try. On the other hand, a press does yield cookies with a distinctive, charming appearance. Certainly if there is already a cookie press in the house, it is fun and rewarding to put it to use. The key to success is to chill the dough just enough so the cookies can be forced through the press plate neatly and hold their shape during baking. Since most presses come with a variety of design plates—such as rosettes, stars, rigid strips, and Christmas trees—it is a good idea to try several and see which ones produce the most attractive results. (Keep in mind, with both piped and pressed cookies, any that do not come out quite right can be scooped up and formed again.) Some Spritz cookies are soft and tender to the point of being cakelike, but these are more on the crisp-tender side.

Using an electric mixer, beat on medium speed until very fluffy and well blended:

½ pound (2 sticks) unsalted butter, softened

¾ cup sugar

Add and beat until well combined:

2 large egg yolks

¼ teaspoon salt

1½ teaspoons vanilla

¾ teaspoon almond extract (optional)

Sift over the top and stir in until well blended and smooth:

2¼ cups all-purpose flour

TO PIPE THE COOKIES:

Stir in:

1½ to 2½ tablespoons milk

until the dough is soft enough to easily force through a pastry bag tube.

Position a rack in the upper third of the oven. Preheat the oven to 350°F. Grease cookie sheets.

Fit the piping bag with a ½-inch-diameter open star (or similar) tip. Fill the pastry bag no more than two-thirds full, twist the opening tightly closed, and squeeze out generous 1½-inch rosettes or stars, spacing about 1 inch apart on the cookie sheets. (For best results, keep the pastry bag and tip perpendicular to the sheet, with the tip almost touching the sheet.)

TO PRESS THE COOKIES:

Do not thin the batter with milk, as it must be slightly firm. If the dough seems soft and difficult to handle, stir in:

1 to 2 tablespoons all-purpose flour

Cover and refrigerate the dough until slightly stiff but not at all hard, 30 to 40 minutes.

Position a rack in the upper third of the oven. Preheat the oven to 350°F. Grease cookie sheets.

To ready the press, insert the desired design plate by sliding it into the head and locking it into place, or follow the manufacturer's instructions. If you are unsure whether the dough is of the right consistency, put a small amount in the press tube and press out several test cookies. Chill the dough further before continuing if it does not go through

cleanly. When the consistency is right, fill the press tube with the dough, packing it down firmly. Press out the cookies, spacing about 1 inch apart on the sheets. Keep the unused dough refrigerated as you work.

If desired, decorate piped or pressed cookies with:

Candied cherry or almond bits, colored sugar sprinkles, or nonpareils

Bake, 1 sheet at a time, until the cookies are just slightly golden and barely tinged with brown at the edges, 9 to 12 minutes. Remove the sheet to a rack and let stand until the cookies firm slightly. Transfer the cookies to racks to cool.

Springerle ❄

2 to 3 dozen assorted 2- to 4-inch cookies

Springerle are striking-looking anise-flavored cookies made by stamping rolled-out dough with carved rolling pins or wooden molds. They are said to come from the old Swabian region of Germany.

Have all ingredients at room temperature, 68° to 70°F. Grease cookie sheets.

Whisk together thoroughly:

3¼ cups all-purpose flour
¼ teaspoon baking powder

Beat on high speed until lightened in color:

4 large eggs

Gradually add and beat until lightened in color, creamy, and thick enough that it drops in thick ribbons, about 3 minutes more:

1⅔ cups sugar
1 teaspoon finely grated lemon zest

1 teaspoon anise extract

Stir in the flour mixture until well blended and smooth. Sprinkle a clean work surface with:

¼ cup all-purpose flour, plus more for the dough

Turn out the dough onto the work surface and sprinkle with a little more flour. Knead in enough flour to firm the dough and make it manageable. Divide the dough in half and place 1 portion in a sealable plastic bag to prevent it from drying out. Roll out the other portion ¼ inch thick, lifting the dough and lightly dusting the work surface and rolling pin as necessary.

Lightly dust a Springerle carved rolling pin or cookie molds with flour; tap off the excess. Firmly roll or press the Springerle rolling pin or molds into the dough to imprint designs. Cut the designs apart using a pastry wheel or sharp knife. With a spatula, transfer the cookies to the cookie sheets, spacing about ½ inch apart. Gather up the dough scraps and knead into the reserved dough. Repeat the rolling and imprinting process until all the dough is used. Set the cookies aside, uncovered, for 10 to 12 hours.

To bake, position a rack in the center of the oven. Preheat the oven to 300°F.

If desired, sprinkle the cookies with:

2 to 3 tablespoons whole or crushed anise seeds

Bake, 1 sheet at a time, until the cookies are almost firm but not colored, 18 to 25 minutes. Transfer the cookies to racks to cool.

DECORATING AND STORING SPRINGERLE

If desired, decorate the cookies by highlighting the designs with a food coloring wash as follows: Dilute vegetable food colorings with a bit of water and, using a small brush, apply a light wash of color to raised areas of the imprint. Or paint the raised areas of the imprint with edible gold leaf (available at specialty baking stores). Let the painted cookies stand until completely dry, about 2 hours. Store airtight for 3 weeks—for a more pronounced anise flavor, add 1 or 2 teaspoons anise seeds to the storage container—or freeze for several months.

Index

Bold type indicates that a recipe has an accompanying photograph.

Almonds
  Austrian Wreaths, 100
  Chocolate Macaroons, 30
  Coconut Macaroons, 28
  Florentines Cockaigne, 32–33
  French Wafers (Tuiles), 35
  Italian Cookies (Amaretti), 31
  Macaroons, 30
  Pretzels (Mandelbrezeln), 72, 86
  Thumbprint Cookies (Reduced Fat), 96, 99
  Tuscan Biscotti (Cantuccini), 87
Amaretti, 31
Angel Bars, 49
Anise Sugar Cookies, Southwest-Style (Biscochitos), 71
Apple Bars, Spiced, 46, 47
Austrian Wreaths, 100

Baking, 10–11
Benne Seed Wafers, 85
Biscochitos, 71
Biscotti
  Chocolate-Coated Mocha, 88, 89
  Classic (Reduced Fat), 88
  Tuscan Almond (Cantuccini), 87
Blondies, 38, 41
Bourbon Balls, 94, 95
Brandied Fruitcake Drops (Reduced Fat), 94, 95
Brandy Snaps, 36, 37
Brownies
  Cheesecake, 44, 45
  Chewy (Reduced Fat), 45
  Cockaigne, 38, 40
  Raspberry Cockaigne, 43
Butter, creaming sugar and, 23
Butterscotch Cookies, 63

Candy Bar Bars, 52
Cantuccini, 87
Cheesecake Brownies, 44, 45
Cherry Pinwheels, Cranberry (Reduced Fat), 106, 107
Chocolate, 42
  Almond Macaroons, 30
  Brownies Cockaigne, 38, 40
  Cheesecake Brownies, 44, 45
  Chewy Brownies (Reduced Fat), 45

  -Cinnamon Cookies, 63
  -Coated Mocha Biscotti, 88, 89
  Florentines Cockaigne, 32–33
  Fudge Drops, Gram Mencke's, 36
  -Glazed Toffee Bars, 50–51
  melting, 51
  Mint Surprises, 103
  Peanut Butter Bars, 53
  Peanut Butter, Chunk Monsters, 27
  Raspberry Brownies Cockaigne, 43
  Rocky Road Bars, 49
  Shortbread, 56, 57
Chocolate Chips
  Classic Cookies, 20, 22
  Congo Bars, 52
  Cookies Cockaigne, 78, 79
  Icebox Cookies, 108, 110
  Mocha Java Congo Bars, 52
  Oatmeal Cookies (Reduced Fat), 22
  Rocky Road Bars, 49
Christmas ornaments, 67
Cinnamon, 24
  -Chocolate Cookies, 63
  Stars, 70
  Sugar Sticks, 92
Cocoa, 42
Coconut
  Almond Macaroons, 28
  Cookies, 63
  Dream (Angel) Bars, 49
  Macaroons, 30
Coffee
  in mocha, see Mocha
  Snaps, 113
Congo Bars, 52
Cookie sheets, see Pans
Cornmeal
  Citrus Cookies, 63
  Cookies, 80
Cranberry Cherry Pinwheels (Reduced Fat), 106, 107
Cream Cheese
  Cheesecake Brownies, 44, 45
  Icebox Cookies, 111
  Peanut Butter Chocolate Bars, 53
  Rugelach, 104, 105
Crescents, Viennese, 82

Decorating, 12–15
Dough, rolling, 65
Dream (Angel) Bars, 49
Drei Augen, 98

Eggs
  beating and folding whites, 29

Florentines Cockaigne, 32–33
Fourteen in One, 62–63
Freezing, 16
French Almond Wafers (Tuiles), 35
Fruitcake Drops, Brandied (Reduced Fat), 94, 95
Fudge Drops, Gram Mencke's, 36

Gazelle's Horns, 102
Gift giving, 16
Ginger
  Cookies, 63
  Orange Wafers (Reduced Fat), 76, 77
  Snaps, 76, 77
Gingerbread
  House, 114–19
  People (Reduced Fat), 66, 67
Glazes
  Honey, 13
  Sugar, 13

Hermits, 25
High-altitude baking, 11
Honey Glaze, 13

Icebox Cookies
  Chocolate Chip, 108, 110
  Cream Cheese, 111
  Sugar, 108, 110
Icings
  Quick, 12
  Quick Lemon, 12
  Royal with Fresh Egg White, 12
  Royal with Powdered Egg White, 12
Ingredients
  choosing, 8
  measuring, 8
  stirring, 43
  substitutions and, 9
  warming, 8
Italian Almond Cookies (Amaretti), 31

Kourambiedes, 84, 85

Lebkuchen, Mother Kroll's, 54, 55
Lemon
  Butter Cookies, 63
  Curd Bars Cockaigne, 46, 47

Glazed Dainties (Reduced Fat), 72, 93
Poppy Seed Cookies, 63
Quick Icing, 12
Linzer Hearts, 96, 98

Macadamia Monsters, White Chocolate, 27
Macaroons
Almond, 30
Chocolate Almond, 30
Coconut, 30
Coconut Almond, 28
Mace, 24
Madeleines, 120
Mandelbrezeln, 72, 86
Marble Cookies, 63
Measuring, 8
Menus, 19
Meringue Nut Kisses (Reduced Fat), 28
Mexican Wedding Cakes, 81
Mint Surprises, Chocolate, 103
Mixing, 8
Mocha
Chocolate-Coated Biscotti, 88, 89
Java Congo Bars, 52
Moravian Molasses Thins, 68, 69

Nutmeg, 24
Nuts
Chocolate-Coated Mocha Biscotti, 88, 89
Dream (Angel) Bars, 49
Meringue Kisses (Reduced Fat), 28
-Orange Cookies, 63
Rocky Road Bars, 49
see also specific nuts

Oatmeal
Chocolate Chip Cookies (Reduced Fat), 22
Classic Cookies, 24
Raisin Monsters, 26
Orange
Butter Cookies, 63
Ginger Wafers (Reduced Fat), 76, 77
-Nut Cookies, 63
Ornaments, 67
Oven
preheating, 10
temperature, 10

Packaging, 16
Palm Leaves, 90, 92

Pans
lining, 41
preparing, 10–11
removing cookies from, 11
types and sizes of, 10
Paper cone, making, 15
Peanut Butter
Chocolate Bars, 53
Chocolate Chunk Monsters, 27
Chubbies, 78
Classic Cookies, 72, 74
Cookies, 63
Pecans
Chocolate-Glazed Toffee Bars, 50–51
Lace, 34
Mexican Wedding Cakes, 81
Tassies, 101
Petticoat Tails, 57
Pfeffernüsse (Peppernuts), 83
Pinwheels, Cranberry Cherry (Reduced Fat), 106, 107
Poppy Seed Cookies, Lemon, 63
Pretzels, Almond (Mandelbrezeln), 72, 86
Puff Pastry
Cinnamon Sugar Sticks, 92
Food Processor, 91
Palm Leaves, 90, 92

Raisins
Classic Oatmeal Cookies, 24
Oatmeal Monsters, 26
-Spice Cookies, 63
Raspberries
Brownies Cockaigne, 43
Streusel Bars, 48
Reduced-fat cookies, 9
Almond Thumbprint Cookies, 96, 99
Brandied Fruitcake Drops, 94, 95
Chewy Brownies, 45
Classic Biscotti, 88
Cranberry Cherry Pinwheels, 106, 107
Gingerbread People, 66, 67
Glazed Lemon Dainties, 72, 93
Meringue Nut Kisses, 28
Oatmeal Chocolate Chip Cookies, 22
Orange Ginger Wafers, 76, 77
Rocky Road Bars, 49
Rolling pins, 65
Royal Icing
with Fresh Egg White, 12
with Powdered Egg White, 12

Rugelach, 104, 105

Sablés, 68, 69
Scottish Shortbread, 56, 57
Sesame (Benne) Seed Wafers, 85
Shipping, 16
Shortbread
Chocolate, 56, 57
Petticoat Tails, 57
Scottish, 56, 57
Snickerdoodles, 75
Spekulatius, 121
Spice Cookies, 63
Springerle, 124, 125
Spritz Cookies, Piped and Pressed, 122, 123
Stirring, 43
Storing, 16
Substitutions, 9
Sugar
creaming butter and, 23
Glaze, 13
syrup, 33
Sugar Cookies
Icebox, 108, 110
Iced, 58, 60
Rich Rolled, 64
Snickerdoodles, 75
Southwest-Style Anise (Biscochitos), 71

Templates, making, 61
Timing, 11
Toffee Bars, Chocolate-Glazed, 50–51
Tuiles, 35
Tuscan Almond Biscotti (Cantuccini), 87
Two Moons, 112

Vanilla, 22
Viennese Crescents, 82

Walnuts
Congo Bars, 52
Fudge Drops, Gram Mencke's, 36
Wedding Cakes, Mexican, 81
White Chocolate Macadamia Monsters, 27

Acknowledgments

Special thanks to my wife and editor in residence, Susan; our friend and editorial assistant, Cynthia Hoskin; and our friends and agents, Gene Winick and Sam Pinkus. Much appreciation also goes to Simon & Schuster, Scribner, and Weldon Owen for their devotion to this project. Thank you Carolyn, Susan, Beth, Rica, Bill, Marah, John, Terry, Roger, Gaye, Val, Norman, and all the other capable and talented folks who gave a part of themselves to the Joy of Cooking All About series.

My eternal appreciation goes to the food experts, writers, and editors whose contributions and collaborations are at the heart of Joy—especially Stephen Schmidt. He was to the 1997 edition what Chef Pierre Adrian was to Mom's final editions of Joy. Thank you one and all.

Ethan Becker

FOOD EXPERTS, WRITERS, AND EDITORS

Selma Abrams, Jody Adams, Samia Ahad, Bruce Aidells, Katherine Alford, Deirdre Allen, Pam Anderson, Elizabeth Andoh, Phillip Andres, Alice Arndt, John Ash, Nancy Baggett, Rick and Deann Bayless, Lee E. Benning, Rose Levy Beranbaum, Brigit Legere Binns, Jack Bishop, Carole Bloom, Arthur Boehm, Ed Brown, JeanMarie Brownson, Larry Catanzaro, Val Cipollone, Polly Clingerman, Elaine Corn, Bruce Cost, Amy Cotler, Brian Crawley, Gail Damerow, Linda Dann, Deirdre Davis, Jane Spencer Davis, Erica De Mane, Susan Derecskey, Abigail Johnson Dodge, Jim Dodge, Aurora Esther, Michele Fagerroos, Eva Forson, Margaret Fox, Betty Fussell, Mary Gilbert, Darra Goldstein, Elaine Gonzalez, Dorie Greenspan, Maria Guarnaschelli, Helen Gustafson, Pat Haley, Gordon Hamersley, Melissa Hamilton, Jessica Harris, Hallie Harron, Nao Hauser, William Hay, Larry Hayden, Kate Hays, Marcella Hazan, Tim Healea, Janie Hibler, Lee Hofstetter, Paula Hogan, Rosemary Howe, Mike Hughes, Jennifer Humphries, Dana Jacobi, Stephen Johnson, Lynne Rossetto Kasper, Denis Kelly, Fran Kennedy, Johanne Killeen and George Germon, Shirley King, Maya Klein, Diane M. Kochilas, Phyllis Kohn, Aglaia Kremezi, Mildred Kroll, Loni Kuhn, Corby Kummer, Virginia Lawrence, Jill Leigh, Karen Levin, Lori Longbotham, Susan Hermann Loomis, Emily Luchetti, Stephanie Lyness, Karen MacNeil, Deborah Madison, Linda Marino, Kathleen McAndrews, Alice Medrich, Anne Mendelson, Lisa Montenegro, Cindy Mushet, Marion Nestle, Toby Oksman, Joyce O'Neill, Suzen O'Rourke, Russ Parsons, Holly Pearson, James Peterson, Marina Petrakos, Mary Placek, Maricel Presilla, Marion K. Pruitt, Adam Rapoport, Mardee Haidin Regan, Peter Reinhart, Sarah Anne Reynolds, Madge Rosenberg, Nicole Routhier, Jon Rowley, Nancy Ross Ryan, Chris Schlesinger, Stephen Schmidt, Lisa Schumacher, Marie Simmons, Nina Simonds, A. Cort Sinnes, Sue Spitler, Marah Stets, Molly Stevens, Christopher Stoye, Susan Stuck, Sylvia Thompson, Jean and Pierre Troisgros, Jill Van Cleave, Patricia Wells, Laurie Wenk, Caroline Wheaton, Jasper White, Jonathan White, Marilyn Wilkenson, Carla Williams, Virginia Willis, John Willoughby, Deborah Winson, Lisa Yockelson.

Weldon Owen wishes to thank the following people for their generous assistance and support in producing this book: Desne Ahlers, Brynn Breuner, Ken DellaPenta, Kyrie Forbes, Arin Hailey, and Norman Kolpas. The photographers wish to thank Champ DeMar, San Francisco; Caruso/Woods, Santa Barbara; Beau Rivage, Santa Barbara; Nancy White; RubyLane.com; and Chrome Works.